Josef Pischl

Distilling Fruit Brandy

with Appendix by Peter Jäger

Disclaimer

The responsibility to comply with all national, state/provincial, and local regulations concerning distilling fruit brandies and producing any other alcoholic beverages lies exclusively with the reader. This includes but is not limited to identifying the responsible government agencies; securing the necessary licenses; processing the appropriate tax forms; procuring and using the approved equipment; following the approved legal processes; and selling, marketing, and distributing according to the law.

The contents of this book have been reviewed by the author and publisher and no guarantees are made regarding the safety, security, and legal risks of following the recipes and procedures herein. The author and publisher assume no legal liability.

Josef Pischl

Distilling Fruit Brandy

Appendix by Peter Jäger

4880 Lower Valley Road • Atglen, PA • 19310

Printed in China

Originally published as *Schnapsbrennen* by Leopold Stocker Verlag, Graz
Translated from the German by Dave Johnston.

Photo credits:
Holstein, pg. 58; Dr. Gardener, University of Innsbruck, pg. 23, 24; IngMauracher, pg. 20, 21; Rider, pg. 115; Schliessmann, pg. 65; Stanzl, pg. 57; Carl C., pg.75 (bottom left), 89; Kothe, pg. 70, 75, 88, 156; Schnapsmuseum Plankenhof, Tyrol, pg. 10, 11, 13, 14, 15, 91, 99, 108, 140; Flora Photo, www.florafoto.de, pg.126 (top and middle), 130; Victoria Ouw Welker-Ling,
www.wedaulink.de, pg. 126 (bottom); Josef Pollhammer, p. 133.The author has provided the rest of the photos as a courtesy.

Disclaimer
The responsibility to comply with all national, state/provincial, and local regulations concerning distilling fruit brandies and producing any other alcoholic beverages lies exclusively with the reader. This includes but is not limited to identifying the responsible government agencies; securing the necessary licenses; processing the appropriate tax forms; procuring and using the approved equipment; following the approved legal processes; and selling, marketing, and distributing according to the law.

The contents of this book have been reviewed by the author and publisher and no guarantees are made regarding the safety, security, and legal risks of following the recipes and procedures herein. The author and publisher assume no legal liability.

Library of Congress Control Number: 2011940672

Designed by Danielle D. Farmer ~ Cover Design by Bruce M. Waters
Type set in ITC Symbol/Bell Gothic

ISBN: 978-0-7643-3926-4 | Printed in China

Published by Schiffer Publishing Ltd.
4880 Lower Valley Road, Atglen, PA 19310
Phone: (610) 593-1777; Fax: (610) 593-2002; E-mail: Info@schifferbooks.com

In Europe, Schiffer books are distributed by
Bushwood Books
6 Marksbury Ave., Kew Gardens, Surrey TW9 4JF England
Phone: 44 (0) 20 8392 8585; Fax: 44 (0) 20 8392 9876
E-mail: info@bushwoodbooks.co.uk; Website: www.bushwoodbooks.co.uk

Contents

Foreword

Alcohol, and especially distilled alcohols, were known to the Egyptians and Greeks. In the Middle Ages, alchemists dealt with the distillation of alcoholic liquids. While they did not find gold, they did create fruit brandies and liquors that cheered the hearts and warmed the stomachs of their fellow men.

Since the first edition of this book was published in 1980, there have been many positive changes in the distillation of fruit brandy. Whereas in the past a fruit brandy was expected to burn, today's consumers expect a particular aroma, which comes from ripe fruit, and smoothness in drinking. A new drinking culture and a new quality consciousness has appeared among both fruit brandy distillers and consumers.

Much has also been learned about the production of top-quality brandies. All of this has been included in this completely revised book. In addition, various terms and designations for measurements have been adapted to the International Units System and EU guidelines.

Once again I have tried to present everything as simply and practically as possible, and I hope that many small licensed distillers will find it useful and produce a good homemade brandy.

Josef Pischl, M. Eng.
Kematen, April 2008

Acknowledgments

Karl Vogl, HR Director, M. Eng., Senior Federal School and Federal Office for Viticulture and Fruit Growing, Klosterneuburg.

He assisted me for many years with his vast knowledge and was always willing to answer my many questions.

Dieter Jenewein, HR Director Mag. and Institute Director Dr. Michael Prean, Austrian Agency for Health and Food Safety GmbH (AGES).

For assisting in the creation of this revised book: Food Code and EU regulations for fruit brandy distillers.

Lambert Draxl, Inzing, and Max Lechner, Rum, both top distillers, for expert consultations and photographic opportunities.

Dr. Ilona Schneider and Amos von Brünning, M. Eng., (both of the Begarow Company) and Dr. Michael Heil (Schließmann Company) for their helpful product advice.

Introduction

The production of fruit brandies is already very old. Improved knowledge and increasingly effective distilling equipment have resulted in steady improvements in alcohol yield and quality. For many decades only windfall fruit and discarded goods were used for distilling. In part this was due to the poor economic situation after WWI and the food shortages during and after WWII. With the economic upturn, the demand for every kind of product rose, including fruit brandy (schnapps).

Today there is a demand for specific-variety brandies, which are supposed to contain the aroma of the variety. In addition to rejects, today there is also economic interest in using table-quality fruit. The manufacture of specialized brandies is often more economically feasible when fruit prices are poor, which is a matter of calculation. This takes some of the burden off the fruit market when there is overproduction. Distillation takes place in the off-season and the distillate is more durable. Good prices can be had if the quality is there; for many small licensed distillers this is an important source of income.

For calculations, it is important that the fruit is weighed and after distillation the alcohol yield per 220 lbs (100 kg) of fruit is determined. This self-checking process is essential for a profitable distillery. If yield is low (e.g. below the official yield figures), the problems must be identified and corrected.

The Basics of Distilling

Fruit brandy is a drink with a high alcohol content. To make it, fruits and roots containing sugar are chopped and mashed. The chopped fruits and roots are called mash.

Fermentation takes place in a vat, with yeast turning the sugar into alcohol. New flavors are created in addition to those already present. In commercial distilleries alcohol is also produced from grain and potatoes. This usually reaches the market in a highly concentrated form. The alcohol yield depends on the sugar content of the initial product and from the degree of distillation. Only ripe, healthy fruits have the required sugar content and the characteristic fruit aroma. Poorly fermented mashes retain some sugar, which of course lowers the alcohol yield. In addition to potable alcohol (ethyl alcohol), the fermentation process creates other substances. Some of these are not suitable for consumption or have an unpleasant taste or smell. The different boiling points of these substances makes it possible to separate them. The boiling point of potable alcohol is about 172.4°F (78°C). The other substances have a lower or higher boiling point. Through careful heating in the still it is possible to separate these substances. To obtain a good distillate, a two-stage distillation process is necessary. If a column is used a single distillation is sufficient.

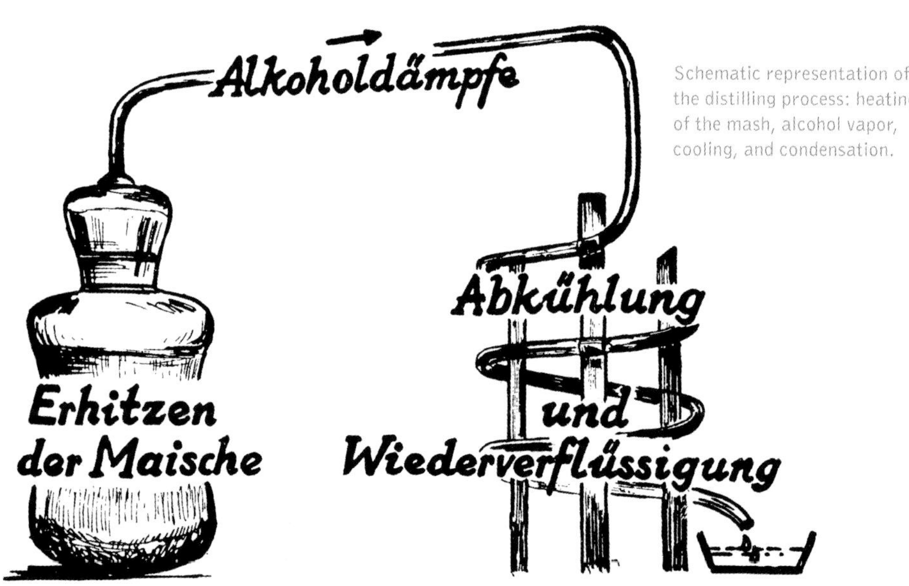

Schematic representation of the distilling process: heating of the mash, alcohol vapor, cooling, and condensation.

The distillation process means that the mash is heated, the alcohol vapor is led to a cooler, and there returned to liquid form (*condensed*). The alcohol thus produced is also referred to as "distillate." The residue from the process is called slop.

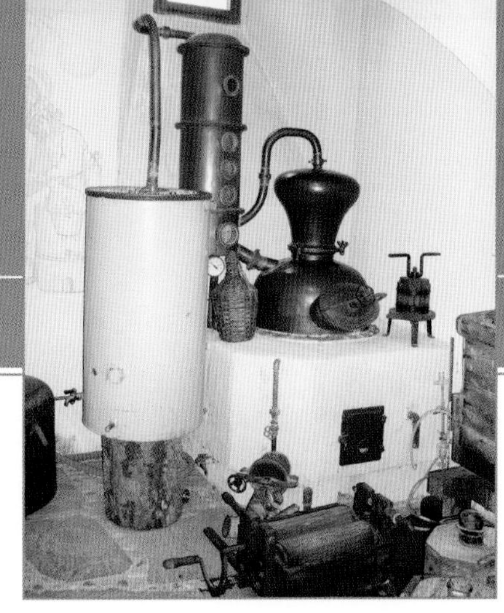

DISTILLATION SCHEME

Crush Fruit – Mash – Fermentation – Distillation

- Simple still (boiler – head – riser pipe – cooler), two distillations are required.

First distillation: the mash produces the low wine, residue in the boiler is called slop.

Second distillation: the low wine produces

- Head: suitable for liniments, not drinkable;
- Heart: potable alcohol (*ethyl alcohol*), good flavor and aroma substances;
- Tail: higher alcohols, bad flavor and aroma substances, not drinkable.

- Stills with enhancement systems (*refinement column*). One distillation is sufficient to separate the head, heart, and tail. For cost reasons, these systems are of interest only if larger quantities of mash are to be distilled. They may have a maximum of three distillation stages (*enhancement plates*) (see pg. 100).

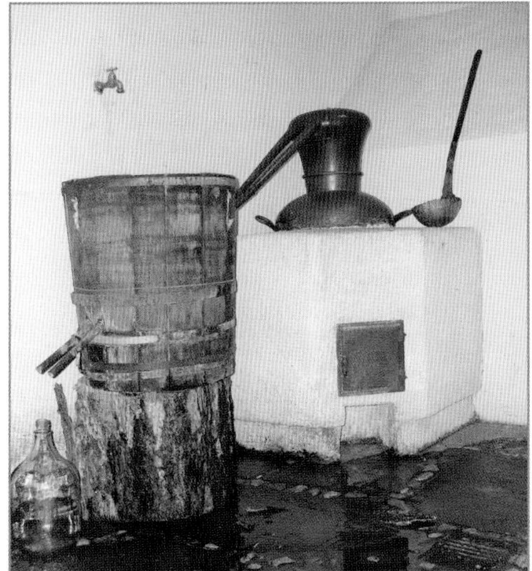

If a simple still is used, two distillation runs are necessary. If the still has an enhancement column, a single distillation is sufficient to separate the head, heart, and tail.

Walled-in, single-wall still with no slop drain and poor cooling.

The Raw Materials of Distilling

Essentially all fruits, roots, and grains containing sugar and starch, plus all liquids containing alcohol can be used to produce alcohol.

Trees such as this one produce inferior fruit for distilling—the fruit contains few sugars and aroma substances.

Here, however, we will only discuss those raw materials, home-grown ones in particular, that are of significance to small, licensed distillers.

The alcohol content depends on the amount of sugar in the fruit, while the fruit's degree of ripeness determines quality. It is therefore of particular importance that the fruit to be used in distilling has achieved full ripeness, for only thus can high sugar content and good aroma be achieved. Basically it is wrong to use lower-quality or incompletely ripened fruit in distilling, as the alcohol yield and quality will not be there. The fruit should be at least completely ripe. Fruit with a low sugar content is better suited for making juice.

The fruit quality begins with care of the tree. Fruit from dense, uncared-for trees will not ripen completely, meaning it is lacking in sugar and aroma. Pruning the trees is therefore necessary, so that sunlight can reach the fruit in the interior of the tree. Sunlight and green, healthy leaves are necessary for the creation of sugar and aroma. In addition, fertilization and a certain degree of plant protection are also beneficial.

FRUITS, BERRIES, AND ROOTS

Water
Quantitatively the greatest part (up to 85%).

Carbohydrates
Mainly various types of sugar, the foundation of alcohol creation.

Other Substances
Acids, protein, minerals etc. In some cases new flavoring substances are produced during the fermentation process.

Flavoring Substances
Of decisive importance in determining distillate quality.

Most varieties of fruits and berries have characteristic flavoring substances. It is important to know that characteristic flavoring substances can only be obtained in full degree from fully ripened fruits. They give the brandy its characteristic aroma. Some varieties develop a unique aroma (e.g. golden delicious, Williams Christ pear). One should take advantage of this fact to produce very special and pure brandies of the highest quality.

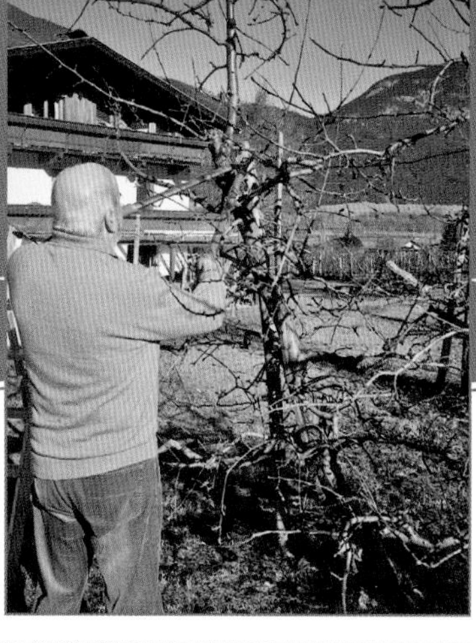

Pruning: the first step towards good quality fruit.

Extract = all dissolved substances in the juice.

Extract

All of the substances contained in fruit form the extract. The main component, however, is sugar, whose precise content cannot be measured easily or quickly. The extract content, however, can be quickly determined (see pg. 26). The extract content is often given as sugar content. This must be taken into consideration when calculating alcohol output, however, meaning that non-sugar elements must be subtracted from the measured extract content (see pg. 30).

Picking Ripeness = Eating Ripeness

GENERAL QUALITY STANDARDS & REQUIREMENTS

With fruit, one must differentiate between picking ripeness and consumption ripeness. In berries (*e.g. elderberries*) and stone fruits (*e.g. apricots*) the two roughly coincide. In the case of pome fruits (*e.g. apples*), especially fall and winter varieties, the two may be separated by weeks or months. It is important for the distiller to know that during the period between picking ripeness and consumption ripeness flavoring substances form in the fruit which are important to the quality of the distillate.

Consumption Ripeness = Mash Ripeness:
Therefore, allow fruit to ripen after picking!

The requirements of good distilling fruit are:

- high sugar content
- consumption ripeness
- marked, varietal aroma
- free of foreign elements like dirt, grass, leaves, etc.

Not suitable for the production of quality brandy are green, rotten, moldy, or poorly formed fruits. They contain little sugar and a low level of aromatic elements.

Fruit for quality brandy.

Trees like this one produce good fruit for distilling.

While fruit such as this will yield some alcohol, it will not result in a quality brandy.

Overripe fruits quickly lose their aroma.

EXCEPTIONS

The Williams Christ pear should be soft when mashed. Overripe damsons and plums produce higher levels of aroma and thus a better quality distillate.

A basic requirement for profitable distilling is a ripe, healthy, and aromatic fruit. Quality brandy comes from quality fruit!

POME FRUITS

In the chapters "Pome Fruits" to "Roots," the stated sugar content always refers to the entire fruit. How close one comes to the higher value depends on the quality of the fruit.

Sugar content varies sharply and depends on the type of fruit, the variety, and especially its state of ripeness.

Well-ripened fruit.

Apples

Classified as table, commercial, and cider apples. All are basically suitable for alcohol production, even selected table and windfall fruit. The sugar content of average quality fruit is between 8 and 12%. The fruit selection actually depends on the desired quality of the product. The quality of apple brandy rises with the quality of the fruit. Top brands require ripe, healthy, and aromatic fruit.

If possible, brandy should be made from a single variety of fruit. Particularly well-suited are: golden delicious, mantet, gravenstein, arlet, jona gold, boskoop, and summer red. Only fully ripe, aromatic fruit should be considered for single-variety brandies, for only thus can the variety's special aroma be transmitted to the distillate.

Early pears are not suited for distillation.

Pears

Table and juice pears are used in distilling, but in far lesser quantities than apples. Sugar content lies between 5 and 12%, with the higher value being seldom attained. Two varieties of pear should be highlighted on account of their outstanding distilling qualities. They are:

Sugar Pear

This is a small, very sweet pear which is also well-suited for dehydration. The yield, unfortunately, is not especially high. This variety of pear is widely used in the Ziller Valley in Tyrol. The resulting brandy has an excellent reputation and is sold under the name "Scheuerbirnenbrand".

Williams Christ Pear

This is an excellent table pear. From it is made the excellent brandy called "Williamsbrand." The variety is very heavy-bearing but has a tendency to scab. In better orchards it pays to plant this variety just for distilling. When fresh fruit prices are good it can be sold; when yields are low or brandy prices are good, use in the distillery is very profitable.

These two varieties should always be mashed and distilled alone.

For pears, too, early varieties are less suitable, as they have less sugar and aroma.

Storage before mashing is necessary, especially when using tannin-rich juice pears, so that the tannin, which can hamper fermentation, can biodegrade.

STONE FRUITS

Sweet Cherries

These produce an outstanding distillate that bears the name "Kirschwasser," literally "cherry water." The dark varieties with dark flesh are especially suitable.

Allow fruit to ripen well. The wild cherry also produces a good brandy. While picking is certainly rather tiring, it is worth it.

Sour Cherries

They are also a good distilling fruit but aren't as ideal for distilling as sweet cherries.

Prune Plums (Damsons)

The best damson brandies are made with so-called "house damsons." When well-ripened, they achieve a high sugar content which can reach 15%. It is difficult to make a precise differentiation between damsons and plums. Basically, damsons are smaller fruits which are pointed at both ends. Damsons should be left on the tree for as long as possible for maximum development of sugar and aroma. The fruit can be allowed to begin withering without concern.

Plums

These fruits are somewhat rounder, the flesh is softer and is more difficult to separate from the stone. Sugar and acid content are somewhat less then that of damsons and the aroma is less marked.

Mirabelle Plums

The mirabelle is a type of plum which is round, yellow and about the size of a cherry. Its flavor is very pleasant and sweet. The high sugar content (up to 15%) ensures a good alcohol yield. Mirabelle brandy is an outstanding and aromatic distillate.

Apricots

Sun-ripened fruit is necessary for a good-quality brandy. Fruit grown in the shade contains less sugar and a weaker aroma. The apricot aroma transfers well to the distillate and is very evident in the brandy.

Peaches

The peach is primarily a consumption fruit and has little significance in brandy making. Peach brandy has a rather weak aroma which is hard to detect.

BERRIES

Black Elderberry

Previously, the only elderberries available for use were from wild plants. As a result of successful plant breeding, however, today several good and heavy-bearing varieties are available. Pure elder brandy has an intense aroma and is easily identifiable as such. An interesting and flavorful brandy can be produced by combining elderberries with apple.

The average sugar content of elderberries is 4-5%, consequently alcohol output is rather low. During the distillation process it is important that the mash be allowed to foam over well. Elderberry brandy has a distinctive taste and is regarded as a specialty brandy (see pg. 129 for more on processing elderberries).

Rowan Berry

One must distinguish between wild Rowan berries found in nature and the cultivated variety, Moravian Rowan berries. Rowan berries come from the mountain ash tree.

The former is a smaller fruit and contains less sugar, but the resulting distillate has a powerful aroma.

The Moravian Rowan berry is a larger berry with a somewhat higher sugar content. Today, pure Vogelbeerbrand (Rowan Berry brandy) is a sought-after distillate.

The true, pure Rowan berry brandy is almost a rarity. Good quality brandy has outstanding taste and aroma and is a popular seller. According to local folklore the brandy has medicinal properties. Harvesting and preparing the fruit for mash is very time-consuming and yield is rather low. The price is therefore also significantly higher than other fruit brandies. Sugar content varies between 4 and 8%.

Every gardener should have at least one mountain ash in his garden.

Juniper Berry

The fruit of the juniper tree is usually sold dried. Sugar content is very high, averaging 20-30% in dried fruit. In addition it contains high levels of resin and essential oils, which give juniper brandy its distinctive aroma and flavor. Pure juniper brandy is rarely drunk today; it is usually diluted with a neutral distillate (see pg. 125).

Raspberry

Unfortunately, raspberries lose much of their delicate flavor during distillation. As they spoil quickly, rapid preparation is necessary. Sugar content varies widely and depending on variety and ripeness ranges between 4 and 7%. As the best fruit is not used (on account of cost), the lower figure is more typical. Distillation should follow soon after fermentation to retain the raspberry aroma.

Raspberries are better suited for the production of spirits (in which the berries are placed in alcohol for several days before distilling, see "Cleaning Distillation" on pg. 125), as this process better preserves the delicate raspberry flavor.

Blueberry

There are cultivated and wild blueberries. The latter are blue throughout and also produce a better aroma.

Currants – Red, Black, White

All three are suitable for making brandy, however, only the black currant is interesting. It produces an intense and distinctive distillate.

Strawberry and Blackberry

Strawberries and blackberries are, of course, suitable for distilling, however they are of little significance.

WILD FRUITS

In addition to cultivated fruits, there are several wild fruits that produce an interesting brandy.

The problem is the sometimes labor-intensive picking of the fruit and its relatively low sugar content. Using simple stills at least three first distillations are necessary to obtain sufficient low wine for a second distillation.

If the amount of fruit available is insufficient for a second distillation, a blended brandy can be made (with apples, for example).

If the fruit yield is low, the low wine can be kept for the next year and processed with the new harvest.

Smaller quantities are practical with a column still, as there is only one distillation run. With a lower alcohol content, double distillation (without enhancement plates) is more advantageous.

Blackthorn (*Sloe*)
Blackthorn is a thorny bush with a small blue, pitted fruit. The effect of frost is necessary to reduce the high tannin content. Little flesh—large stone volume—low alcohol output. (*See illustration* ↑)

Cornel Cherry
The cornel cherry is an ornamental shrub with red fruit. The fruit must be fully ripe before harvesting. The low acid content makes acidification necessary to achieve proper fermentation. (*See illustration* →)

Black Cherry
The black cherry is another fruit found on trees in the wild. The fruit is black and grows on long stalks. The stones are large and the percentage of flesh low, consequently alcohol output is low.

Other wild fruits include the service tree berry, which is found in sunny regions, and the hawthorn berry, which is found at the edges of woods and forests.

ROOTS

Gentian Root
Of these, however, the yellow gentian is most widely used in distilling.

The following varieties of gentian are found in the Alpine nations:

Yellow Gentian – *Gentiana lutea*
Spotted Gentia – *punctata L.*
Purple Gentian – *Gentiana purpurea*
Pannonic Gentian – *Gentiana pannonica L.*

If one wishes to dig the roots himself, he will of course have to

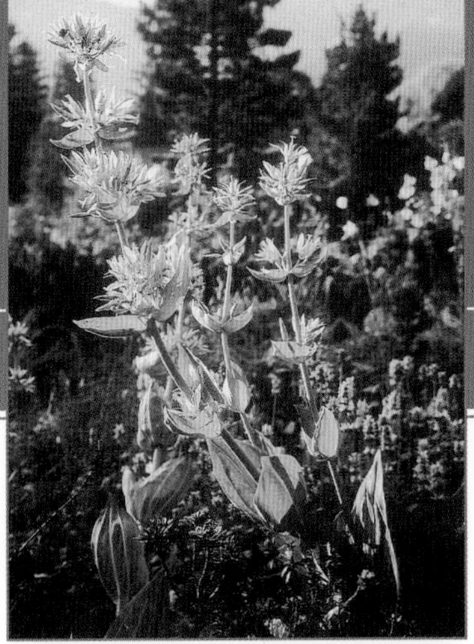

abide by conservation laws. In many areas these varieties of gentian are protected. A permit to dig can be obtained from the responsible authorities (District Administrative Authority, Austria). It is important that all holes be filled, so that the remaining roots can spread. The result is a rejuvenation of the stock. This is why the total ban on digging was lifted.

The roots can be used fresh or dried. The sugar content of fresh roots is about 7–16%; in dried roots this figure can be as high as 30%. It is the bitterns in the roots which give gentian brandy its characteristic taste.

Masterwort (*Imperatoria struthium L.*)
The masterwort is a wild-growing mountain plant that belongs to the carrot family. The roots are used for distilling. The brandy is said to be very good for the stomach. It has a delicate aroma and these days is often preferred over gentian brandy.

The roots can be used fresh or dried. If one wishes to dig the roots himself, he will of course have to abide by conservation laws (*permits are available from the District Administrative Authority, Austria*). (*See Gentian.*)

Turnip
Only in the Wildschonau, a side-valley near Wörgl in Tyrol, may this turnip variety be distilled commercially. The right to do so was granted to the inhabitants by Maria Theresa in the eighteenth century. The resulting brandy bears the name "Krautinger." Opinions vary sharply about its distinctive flavor. Opinions aside, a good Krautinger is an interesting schnapps. Preparation is very time consuming and prone to errors; quality is not always what is desired.

FRUIT WINE AND MUST

Grape Wine

Alcohol content is usually between 9 and 12% by volume. Wine is well-suited for distilling. The distilled wine produced from mashed fruit or grape wine is called brandy (Weinbrand). The extent to which wine is distilled these days is usually a matter of calculation. Direct sales of good wines are certainly more profitable. Wine from private gardens and various wine residues can, however, be employed profitably.

Fruit Wine or Must

In general the entire fruit is mashed and distilled. The pome fruits (apples and pears), however, can be pressed first and the juice fermented to make fruit wine. The distilling of fruit wine is certainly somewhat simpler, especially with single-wall stills, although the flavor of the resulting distillate is altered somewhat.

In France the famous Calvados is made from fruit wine. The ripe, clean fruit is pressed, strained through a cloth and emptied into clean barrels. The recipe calls for one half of a potassium pyrosulfite tablet (dissolved in water) per hectoliter and pure yeast to be added. A tenth of the barrel volume is left as fermentation space. The barrel is sealed with an airlock. Fermentation is completed in three weeks at a temperature of 64.4°F (18°C). The applicable regulations must be followed when distilling must. Alcohol output depends on the quality of the fruit and reaches 6% on average. The must is especially suited for distilling in single-wall stills, as it cannot catch fire.

If one uses poor quality fruit wine for distilling, one must naturally expect a poor-quality distillate. Acetic-tainted fruit wines are particularly bad, as the acetic acid is transferred to the distillate with the alcohol. A must of this kind must first be de-acidified or processed into vinegar.

Fruit and Grape Wine Sediment

This is the residue left by fermentation, consisting of dead yeast, debris, and some wine. It should only be used fresh, as long as the yeast has not spoiled.

The sediment foams vigorously during distillation and can easily spill over into the cooler, therefore exercise caution when distilling! As certain odor and flavor elements are retained during distillation, it is better to put the sediment in a heavy sack, press it and use the recovered juice for distilling.

Fruit or Wine Pomace

Fruit or wine pomace can be fermented and then distilled. The average alcohol yield from fruit pomace is 3/8 to 1/2 gallon (1 1/2 to 2 liters) of alcohol per 220 lbs (100 kg) of pomace. In the case of wine pomace the yield depends on the previous extraction of the pomace.

Extract Value

Equipment for Measuring Extract Levels

Calculating the Sugar Content of Fruit Juice

Calculating the Sugar Content of Mash

Determining Probable Alcohol Yield

Probable Alcohol Yield

Prior to mashing, one should have some idea of the expected alcohol yield so that an appropriate selection of fruit can be made.

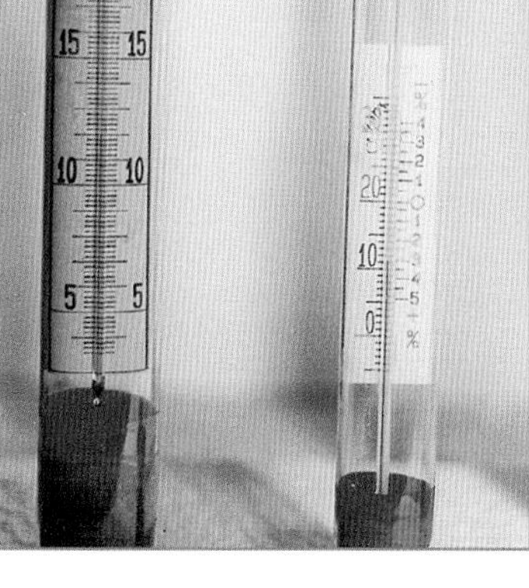

Prior to mashing, one should have some idea of the expected alcohol yield so that an appropriate selection of fruit can be made.

In the fruit juice, the dissolved elements form the "extract." The sugar content can be determined from the contents of the extract.

The following substances are dissolved in the juice:	
SUGAR	used by the yeast to create alcohol
Fruit acid Tannin Proteins Vitamins Mineral compounds Flavoring substances	these are non-sugar substances,some form flavoring substances but no alcohol

EXTRACT VALUE

Definition of %mas

Today extract value is expressed internationally in %mas (percent mass) = g extract/100 g or dekagram (dag)/kg.

The old name for this term is wt% (weight percent). But it is still popular today.

% mas = wt%

EQUIPMENT FOR MEASURING EXTRACT LEVELS

In small distilleries the saccharometer (*from Brix or Plato*), the wine refractometer, and the hand refractometer are used to determine extract levels.

Extract measurement: 13 %mas extract.

Saccharometer

This is a hydrometer which is calibrated in a water-sugar solution at a specific temperature (normally 68°F [20°C]). The calibration temperature is given on the saccharometer and the juice to be measured should be at this temperature in order to obtain accurate readings. Because the extract consists mainly of sugar, the values are often expressed as sugar content percentage, however, this is too imprecise for calculating alcohol yield. The non-sugar elements must be taken into consideration.

Use

- Use a saccharometer with a built-in thermometer!
- The saccharometer and measuring cylinder must be clean and free of grease.
- The liquid to be measured must be free of solids.
- The temperature of the juice must be the same as the calibration temperature (*correct if necessary).*
- If air bubbles form on the saccharometer, remove it from the liquid and carefully insert it again.

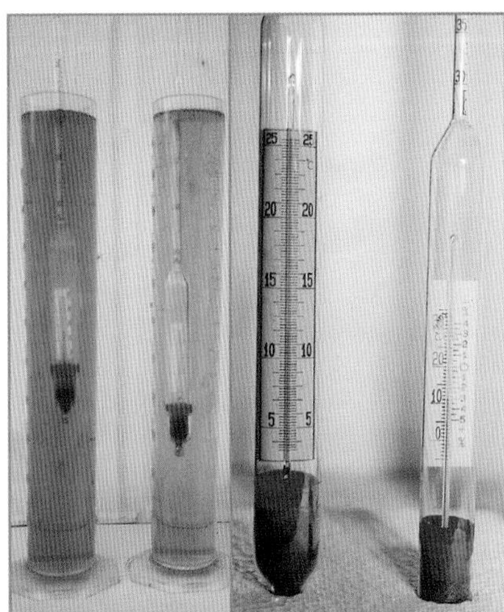
Saccharometer with thermometer: (center) spindle sinks deep, fermented; (left) spindle partly submerged, unfermented.

- There are two methods of taking readings. Unless stated otherwise on the saccharometer, the reading is taken from the bottom. If the reading is to be taken from the top, this will be marked on the meter.
- Temperature variations must be taken into account. 0.06% is added for each degree above the desired temperature, and 0.06% is subtracted for each degree below.

Wine Refractometer

This hydrometer measures the density of a liquid. The more substances dissolved in a liquid, the greater its density. It functions in the same way as a saccharometer. A refractometer with built-in thermometer should be used to enable temperature corrections to be made.

Temperature correction

If temperature is over, 0.02° Öchsle* is added for each degree Centigrade. If temperature is under, 0.02° Öchsle is subtracted for each degree Centigrade.

** The Öchsle is a unit used in Germany and Switzerland to measure the density of must. One degree Oechsle is roughly equivalent to 0.2% sugar by weight.*

Conversion to Saccharometer Percentage

$$\frac{\text{Öchsle Degree}}{4} = \text{saccharometer percentage}$$

Refractometer

Measurement with a refractometer is an optical method. Measurement requires only a few drops of juice, which must be free of solids. Several measurements should be taken to obtain an accurate average. Measurements should be taken according to the directions for use.

Refractometer for quick extract measurement.

The refractometer has the advantage of being able to take numerous measurements in a short time.

The extract values in the table on page 29 are approximate values and say nothing about the extract content of the various fruits. This can only be determined by testing the extract with a refractometer or saccharometer.

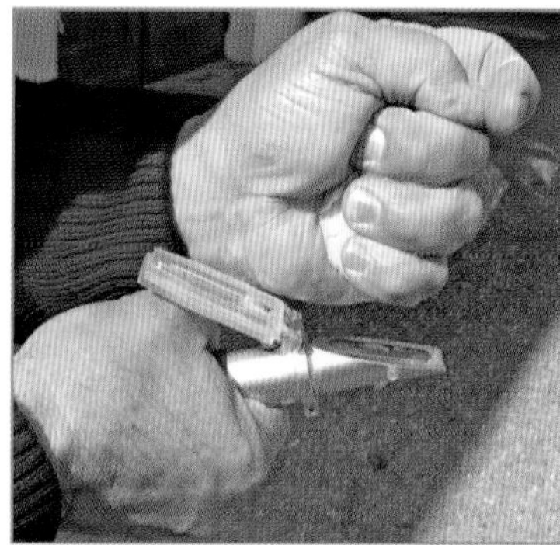
Squeeze out juice for extract measurement.

Extract measurement with refractometer.

Refractometer.

HBP Extract Contents of Unfermented Fruit Mashes

MATERIAL	SACCHAROMETER (from PLATO) (%mas)	MUST WEIGHT (Calibration Temp. = 20°C) (Must weight)	SOURCES & NOTES
Apples, pears; no specific variety	12-17	48-68	Windisch/Rüdiger/Schwarz/Malsch (1965)
Table apples (11 varieties)	11-16	44-64	Röhrig/Pieper (1982, 1983)
Table Apples by Variety James Grieve Gravenstein Jona Gold Jonathan Boskoop Red Delicious Golden Delicious	12-14 (10-11) 10-14 (12-16) 11-15 12-17 14-15 11-17	48-56 40-56 44-60 48-68 55-60 44-68	Röhrig/Pieper (1982) as well ongoing research from 1975 to 1980 by the Department of Fermenting Technology of the University of Hohenheim with fruit from the same. The values in brackets go back to Muller and Schobinger (1974).
Must Pears (9 varieties)	14-17	56-68	Röhrig/Pieper (1979)
Table Pears (11 varieties)	10-16	10-16	Röhrig/Pieper (1982, 1983)
Williams Christ Pears	9-14	40-56	Kolb (1973); Nosko (1974); Röhrig/Pieper (1982, 1983)
Cherries	13-22	52-88	Windisch/Rüdiger/Schwarz/Malsch (1965)
Sour Cherries (14 varieties)	10-17	40-68	Pieper/Graf (1985)
Damsons	10-20	40-80	Windisch/Rüdiger/Schwarz/Malsch (1965)
Plums	10-15	40-60	Windisch/Rüdiger/ Schwarz/Malsch (1965)
Mirabelle Plums	16-18	64-72	Windisch/Rüdiger/Schwarz/Malsch (1965)
Raspberries, Blueberries, Blackberries	8-10	32-40	Windisch/Rüdiger/Schwarz/Malsch (1965)
Rowan Berries	15-25	60-100	Windisch/Rüdiger/Schwarz/Malsch (1965)
Elderberries	8-11	32-44	Windisch/Rüditer/Schwarz/Malsch (1965)

CALCULATING THE SUGAR CONTENT OF FRUIT JUICE

Sugar content = extract less non-sugar substances.

The values obtained with a saccharometer or refractometer reveal the extract content. After removing the non-sugar substances (Nz), one obtains the approximate sugar content.

These are average values; there will be differences depending on the variety of fruit and degree of ripeness.

Approximate Values of Non-Sugar Substances

TYPE OF FRUIT	NON-SUGAR SUBSTANCES IN THE JUICE
Apples	2.5%
Pears	3.5%
Blackberries	3.5%
Strawberries	3.5%
Blueberries	3.5%
Raspberries	3.5%
Currants	3.5%
Gooseberries	3.5%
Damsons	4.0%
Cherries	5.0%
Rowan Berries	7.0%

% sugar = % extract – non-sugar substances = % E – Nz

$$\% \text{ sugar} = \frac{°\text{Öchsle}}{4} - \text{Nz}$$

Example

Apple juice with 11.5 °mas Extract (E)
Non-sugar substances (Nz) for apples 2.5 °mas
E – NZ = 11.5 – 2.5 = 9 %mas sugar in the juice (*mas stands for percent by mass*)

CALCULATING THE SUGAR CONTENT OF MASH

Sugar content is critical in determining alcohol yield.

One must take into account the amount of residue in the mash.

Raw Material	Residue Content (Tg) in the Mash	Residue Factor (T)
Apples	6-8%[1]	0.92-0.94
Pears	8-10%[1]	0.90-0.92
Damsons	11-12%[1]	0.88-0.89
Cherries	15%[1]	0.85
Varieties of Table Apples		
Gravenstein	3.0%[2]	0.97
James Grieve		
Boskoop		
Cox		
Golden Delicious	3.5%[2]	0.965
Goldparmäne		
Jonathan	4.0 %	0.96
[1]*Estimated Value*	[2]*Measured Value*	

The lower value should be applied to well-developed and ripened fruit.

Example

The sugar content of our juice is 9%, the assumed residue component (T) is 6%, the factor 0.94%.

Sugar in the mash = sugar in the juice × 0.94 = 9 x 0.94 = **8.46 %mas**.

DETERMINING PROBABLE ALCOHOL YIELD

Theoretically, 220 lbs (100 kilograms) of sugar will yield 17 gallons (64.5 liters) of alcohol. Some loss results from processing, however, and a more typical yield is 14.5 gallons (55 liters).

Alcohol yield per 100 l of mash = sugar content × 0.55

Example

Our apple mash has 8.46 %mas of sugar.
Alcohol per 100 l of mash = 8.46 x 0.55 = 4.65 l
This mash should be able to yield **4.65 total liters of alcohol** (*first, second, and final runs*).

The calculated alcohol yield is a guideline. If the actual alcohol yield is significantly less than anticipated, the reason for this should be found (fermentation stopped, poor fermentation, incorrect measurements used in calculations, etc.). This calculated 4.65 liters (1 1/4 gallons) of alcohol is based on the head, heart, and tail. The realizable quantity of distillate from the middle-run is correspondingly lower and is based on the necessary fore- and after-runs.

Calculated alcohol yield can only be achieved through proper preparation.

Fermentation Vessels

Cleaning Fermentation Vessels

Fermentation Vessels and Their Care

A wide variety of containers can be used as fermentation vessels, provided they meet certain requirements. They must be capable of being cleaned, for any contamination can spoil the mash. They should also have an opening sufficiently large to allow the mash to be put in and removed. A larger opening is also advantageous for cleaning.

The container material must be of a type that is not attacked by the mash or influences its flavor. As well, it must not allow harmful substances to leach into the mash.

Stainless steel and plastic containers, in particular, meet all these requirements. It is important that the mash never remain in contact with bare metal parts (especially iron and aluminum) for long periods, with the exception of stainless steel. In some cases the acids in the fruit attack the metal, resulting in flawed distillates.

FERMENTATION VESSELS

Plastic

Plastic containers are made of low-pressure polyethylene and fiberglass-reinforced polyester resin. Containers are available in sizes of 30 to 220 liters (~8 to 55 gallons) and consequently are very popular among commercial distillers and owners of raw materials. There are of course larger containers.

Their advantages are:

- low weight
- high stability
- easy cleaning of smooth inner surfaces
- large filler opening
- easy to transport even when full
- tight-fitting cover
- long life

In other types of plastic containers the alcohol can release substances that can alter the flavor of the contents.

If buying used containers, check to ensure that there is no residual odor from the previous contents. If there is, the container is unsuitable, as the odor will be transferred to the mash during fermentation and will, of course, be retained by the distillate.

For the storage of low wine only use containers that are suitable for holding alcohol, and do not use for high-percentage distillate.

Metal

Rustproof stainless steel (e.g. V2A, V4A) is an ideal material for metal containers. It is acid-resistant, has an odor- and taste-neutral behavior towards the contents and is completely airtight. Stainless steel containers are also best for storage of high-percentage distillate and are affordable.

Stainless steel containers.

CLEANING FERMENTATION VESSELS

Because of their smooth surfaces, plastic and stainless steel containers are easy to clean; lukewarm water and a soft brush will suffice. Very dirty containers should be filled with water and left to sit for several days before cleaning. All fermentation containers with an inner lining should be cleaned in such a way that the liner is not damaged. The companies that make such linings have also published instructions for the cleaning of their products.

Anyone who prefers order will clean the container as soon as it is emptied and stand it up with the opening facing down. After the container has dried, the cover is put on, and it is stored until needed again.

A high-pressure cleaning apparatus is excellent for cleaning containers.

Mash fermentation vessels with required markings (vessel number in Roman numerals and vessel contents in Arabic numbers).

Agent of Fermentation

Other Fermentation Agents

Presence of Yeasts

Process of Fermentation

Products of Fermentation

Influence of Temperature on Fermentation

Alcoholic Fermentation

The fermentation that takes place in fresh fruit and fruit juice was known to most ancient peoples. Until approximately the nineteenth century, people knew little about the processes that takes place during fermentation or its causes and agents until Louis Pasteur (1822–1895) discovered that yeast was the agent of fermentation.

AGENT OF FERMENTATION

Pure Yeasts

Yeasts are single-cell microbes belonging to the mushroom group. Their average diameter is 0.004 to 0.014 mm. After the discovery of yeast, it was soon learned that there are differences among yeasts and that the individual strains of yeast behave very differently in terms of fermentation strength and other characteristics. After much painstaking work, pure cultures were raised from single yeast cells, and their fermentation qualities were closely examined. The best strains are now sold commercially as pure selected yeast or pure yeast.

Left: yeast cells;
a) mother cell, b) shoot

Center: yeast bud chain

Right: budding yeast

(from H. Walter, Basics of Plant Life)

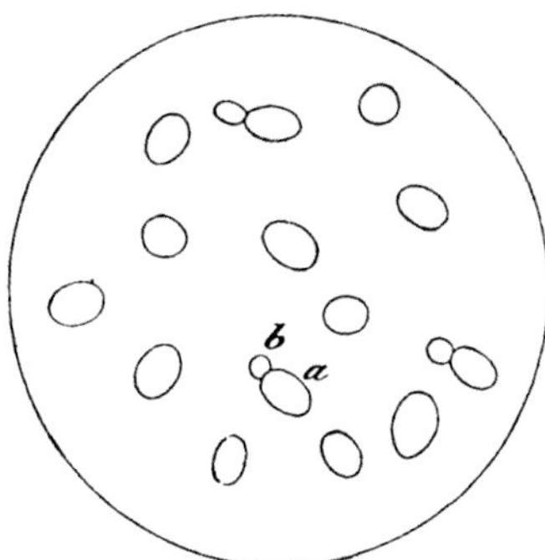

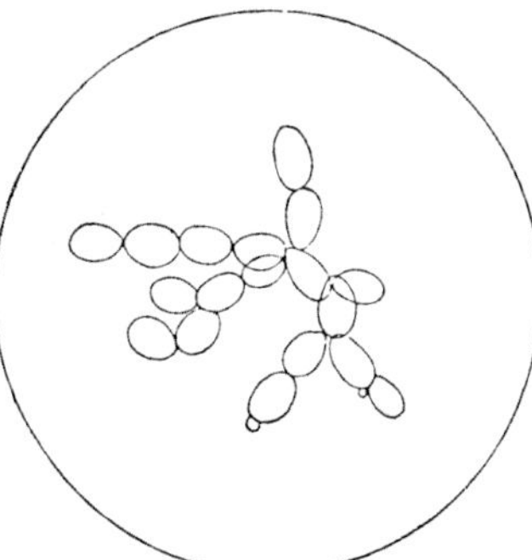

Nowadays there are strains of yeast that produce good flavor and bouquet substances during fermentation.

Purpose of Pure Selected Yeast

Pure selected yeast turns sugar into alcohol.

Pure selected yeast transforms the entire sugar content into alcohol, creates good flavor and aroma substances, completes the alcohol creation process quickly, and forms no undesirable by-products. There are also special strains, such as cold yeasts (*Kaltgärhefen*), that will work at temperatures as low as 41°F (5°C). One must remember, however, that these cold yeasts work much more slowly, meaning that complete fermentation of a mash will take much longer. Even when using cold yeast, one should strive for a fermentation temperature of 59-64.4°F (15-18°C) to ensure that fermentation proceeds quickly.

OTHER FERMENTATION AGENTS

Other kinds of yeast can spoil a mash.

There are other strains of yeast such as Apiculatus yeast and Kahm yeast. They produce little alcohol and also destroy valuable elements of the mash. If air enters the container, Kahm yeast often produces a thick, grey, wrinkly skin on the surface of the mash. This causes the fermentation product (wine, mash) to lose quality. These fermentation agents are undesirable and their development must be suppressed through proper fermentation methods (use of pure selected yeast, proper container closure).

PRESENCE OF YEASTS

Natural yeasts are present everywhere.

Yeasts are present everywhere in nature and on all fruits, like apples, pears, and berries. In addition to true yeasts, Kahm yeasts, bacteria, molds, and other microorganisms are also present. The addition of pure yeast will inhibit the growth of the many undesired microbes in the mash. One must be aware, however, that the presence of wild yeasts in nature is largely dependent on the weather. During cold, damp autumn weather the amount of yeast present on fruit is much lower, so fermentation would be delayed without the addition of pure yeast.

Spontaneous Fermentation

So-called spontaneous fermentation is caused by "wild yeast" present on fruits in nature. The fermentation process begins more slowly, however, giving other (undesirable) microorganisms on the fruit a chance to develop. Fermentation is not impaired until oxygen levels drop and alcohol levels rise, but by then undesirable substances, such as acetic acid or bad flavor or odor substances, may have formed. This undesirable process can be hindered through the addition of pure yeast.

Wild yeast—fermentation begins more slowly.

PROCESS OF FERMENTATION

At a temperature of 68°F (20°C) the yeast multiplies very rapidly. It contains an enzyme complex called Zymase, which ferments the fructose and dextrose into alcohol and carbon dioxide. Other substances are also formed. Fermentation should take place in a sealed container to keep the air out.

As the yeast multiplies, it rapidly uses up the oxygen in the mash. As a result, the development of all microorganisms that live on oxygen is slowed or halted.

Growth of oxygen-dependent organisms is hampered or stopped.

The development of other microorganisms is checked by the rapid production of alcohol. This permits a clean fermentation by the pure selected yeast.

As it is formed, the carbon dioxide rises through the mash, mixing it in the process. The free space above the mash fills with carbon dioxide, which forces out the oxygen, and then escapes through the airlock.

Fermentation Equation

$C_6H_{12}O_6$ >	$2C_2H_5OH$ +	$2CO_2$
Fructosepotable Dextrose	Alcohol Ethyl Alcohol	Carbon Dioxide
100g	51g	49g

Fermentation Phases

They can be divided into three segments:

Prefermentation

Large increase in the number of yeast cells through the oxygen content of the mash and little alcohol formation.

Primary Fermentation

Intensive fermentation activity takes place during this phase. Large amounts of carbon dioxide and alcohol are formed. This phase is also called “vigorous fermentation.” It is accompanied by a rise in temperature.

Observe the airlock to follow the progress of fermentation.

Secondary Fermentation

Most of the sugar has been consumed, little carbon dioxide production.

These three phases can easily be monitored by observing the airlock:

Prefermentation – little discharge of carbon dioxide
Primary Fermentation – heavy discharge of carbon dioxide
Secondary Fermentation – diminishing discharge of carbon dioxide

Observation of the airlock makes it possible to follow the fermentation process and immediately detect possible problems.

PRODUCTS OF FERMENTATION

Alcohol

The most important product of the fermentation process is potable alcohol (ethyl alcohol). The amount produced depends on the sugar content of the fermentation liquid or mash. It is lighter than water (1 liter weighs 790 g [1/4 gallon weighs 1 3/4 lbs]) and boils at 172.4°F (78°C). In addition to potable alcohol, "higher-order alcohol" or fusel oil, is also produced.

Undesirable substances are produced in addition to potable alcohol.

Glycerin

Glycerin is an oily, sweet-tasting liquid. One liter of wine contains approximately 6 to 9g (~1/4 oz to 2/3 oz) of glycerin. The glycerin in the wine and the mash is desirable as it makes the wine more full-bodied. During distillation glycerin is not transferred to the distillate.

Carbon Dioxide (CO_2)

CO_2 is created in large quantities during fermentation. It is heavier than air and has an asphyxiating action. Fermentation cellars must be provided with adequate ventilation in order to remove the gases produced during fermentation. When entering a fermentation cellar, one should always take a lit candle and place it at working height. If the candle burns poorly or goes out (without a draft), leave the cellar immediately, there is a danger of asphyxiation. As the CO_2 rises, it causes a vigorous upheaval of the mash.

The CO_2 also fills the open space above the mash in the fermentation vessel. This forces the oxygen out of the vessel, making it impossible for oxygen-dependent microorganisms (acetic acid bacteria, Kahm yeast, etc.) from developing. As CO_2 is heavier than air, it remains lying on top of the mash. This layer of CO_2 should not be disturbed, in order to prevent oxygen from again reaching the mash.

Acetaldehyde

Acetaldehyde is a natural by-product of distillation. Acetaldehyde content increases sharply when the fermentation process is poor. Its boiling point is roughly 68°F (20°C), therefore it can easily be removed through proper heating of the mash. It has a pungent odor and taste and is undesirable in the finished distillate.

Acetaldehyde: typical fore-run product—easily removable.

Fusel Oils

These are higher-order alcohols with boiling points of 176-320°F (80-160°C). They have an unpleasant smell and taste and are not desired in the final distillate. If the alcohol concentration is lower than 42% during second distillation, the higher-order alcohols are more rapidly transferred to the distillate. One should therefore proceed to final distillation on a timely basis.

Methanol (Methyl Alcohol)

Enzymes in the fruit transform pectin into methanol. It is poisonous, has an odor similar to alcohol and a boiling point of 166.5°F (74.7°C). There is no satisfactory method of removing methanol, consequently it is present in the fore-, middle-, and after-runs. Methanol is poisonous to humans, consequently there are maximum levels for finished brandies that must not be exceeded.

Methanol is poisonous to humans—be aware of maximum allowable levels.

Fruit Brandies: 2.2 lbs/26.4 gallons (1000 grams/100 liters of alcohol)

Exceptions are: apples, pears (excluding Williams), damsons, plums, mirabelles, raspberries, and blackberries; for these the maximum limit is 2.6 lbs per 26.4 gallons (1200 g per 100 liters) of alcohol.

2.9 lbs per 26.4 gallons (1350 grams per 100 liters) of alcohol: Williams Christ pears, quinces, black elder, currants (black and red), Rowan berries, juniper berries.

Aroma and Flavor Substances

In addition to the aroma and flavor substances in the fruit, good strains of yeast produce new aroma and flavor substances which are indispensable for a good quality distillate. If the fermentation process is less than satisfactory, however, these substances cannot form in sufficient quantity or quality.

Optimal fermentation process reduces undesirable substances.

Other Substances

Bad aroma and flavor substances, acetic acid etc., are formed in small quantities even in good distillation processes. If the initial product is poor or the fermentation process is less than satisfactory, however, these products can increase rapidly, resulting in a poor quality distillate.

Optimal mash temperature for good fermentation: 64.4-68°F (18-20°C).

INFLUENCE OF TEMPERATURE ON FERMENTATION

A certain amount of heat is released by the fermentation process, meaning that the contents of larger containers heat up. The ideal fermentation temperature is 64.4-68°F (18-20°C). Higher temperatures are less desirable, as yeast ceases fermentation activity at 104°F (40°C) and dies at 140°F (60°C). When using smaller quantities of fruit, care must be taken to ensure that the mash temperature is at least 64.4°F (18°C) when fermentation begins. The fruit must therefore always be sufficiently warm when mashed (64.4-68°F [18-20° C]).

While low-temperature yeast will work even at lower temperatures (to 41°F [5°C]), it works more slowly as temperature falls. In order to achieve rapid fermentation, one should strive for a temperature of 59-64.4°F (15-18°C) even with cold yeast.

Excessively high fermentation temperatures are to be avoided, as they can result in loss of aroma and alcohol.

Williams Christ pears, for example, should not be fermented at over 64.4°F (18°C).

Types of Pure Selected Yeast

Preparation and Use of Yeast (*Yeast Pitching*)

Pure Selected Yeast and Its Use

In addition to wild yeasts, many other microorganisms are also present on fruit. These can multiply in the mash and in some cases produce unwanted substances.

Vacuum-packed dry yeast

The development of many microorganisms is not impeded until the wild yeast has multiplied sufficiently and produced alcohol and CO_2. The unwanted substances that have formed by then, which can affect the quality of the distillate, of course remain. If one adds pure selected yeast immediately upon mashing according to the directions for use, the yeast takes over, so to speak, and the development of the remaining microorganisms is very quickly checked. This also results in a pure distilled product.

Pure selected yeast is the most important mash additive.

It is responsible for a rapid initiation of fermentation, a clean, smooth fermentation, and an optimal alcohol yield.

Scientific research has led to great advances in the field of pure selected yeast. The first pure selected yeasts were developed to produce a quick, clean, smooth fermentation. Since then, scientists have developed warm and cold yeasts, yeasts that ferment slowly or quickly, which are neutral or increase aroma, and even some that produce specific aromas.

Undoubtedly there will be further advances in selected yeasts. It is worth the effort to experiment with new strains.

TYPES OF PURE SELECTED YEAST

Dry Yeast – powder or granules
Liquid Yeast
Pressed Yeast

Dry Yeast

At present, dry selected yeast is the most commonly used type of yeast.

During the manufacture of dry selected yeast the water is carefully removed. Specially packaged, it is sold in various sizes, 100 and 500 grams being typical. Opened packets should be sealed rapidly and stored in a refrigerator. Packet size should be chosen so that opened packets do not have to be stored for more than a year. Dry yeast is viable for three years after the production date. Pay attention to the production and expiry dates when purchasing.

Dry yeast.

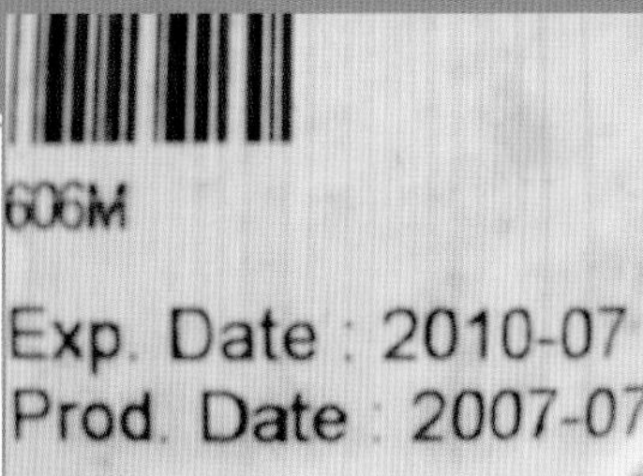

606M
Exp. Date : 2010-07
Prod. Date : 2007-07

Production and expiry dates on a yeast packet.

Each gram of dry yeast contains 20-25 million yeast cells. If improperly stored for long periods, the yeast cells will die or become damaged.

Liquid Yeast
Scarcely used any more, even specialist shops no longer carry it. Liquid yeast can only be obtained from relevant teaching and research facilities.

Pressed Yeast (*Baking Yeast*)
This type is especially suitable for fermenting Rowan berries, juniper berries, and gentian root. Add 300-500 grams per hectoliter of mash. The starting temperature of the mash should be about 75.2°F (24°C) as pressed yeast requires higher temperatures than wine yeast.

When using pure selected yeast, always follow the instructions! At present dry yeast is the simplest to use.

PREPARATION AND USE OF YEAST (*YEAST PITCHING*)

Dry yeast must be brought to life again.

Placing the yeast in plain water is ineffective as the necessary nutrients are not present. As well, once mixed with water the yeast must be used within 15-20 minutes.

Adding the yeast to fruit juice or mash is also undesirable, as the sugar concentration is too high. Optimal regeneration is possible in neither case. The best solution is a water/fruit juice or water/mash mixture in a ratio of 1 : 1. Temperature should be 95°F (35° C) (*measure*).

If several vessels are to be mashed, an appropriate quantity of startup yeast should be prepared.

Stirring the dry yeast into a warm (95°F [35°C]) juice-water mixture.

Foam buildup—the yeast has multiplied greatly.

Adding yeast to a mash-water mixture.

Example

Five, 26.4-gallon (100-liter) vessels are to be mashed. The necessary quantity of yeast is prepared (according to the directions on the packet). We want to add 4 1/4 cups (1 liter) of startup yeast to each vessel.

Place 2/3 gallon (2.5 liters) of fruit juice or mash in a suitable container and top up with hot water to 1 1/3 gallon (5 liters). Temperature should be 95°F (35°C) (measure). Using a whisk, stir in the appropriate amount of yeast, ensuring that no lumps remain. Now the yeast has sufficient nutrients for many hours. Allow the yeast to slowly cool to the temperature of the fruit (important). One liter of startup yeast is then removed and added in portions via the mash mill or stirred into the vessel.

Quick Guide

- Prepare yeast
- Mix one part fruit juice or mash with one part hot water—35°C (95°F) starting temperature
- Stir yeast with whisk to remove lumps
- Let stand until yeast reaches temperature of fruit.

**Cold yeast in warm water (95°F [35°C]) causes no harm.
Pouring warm yeast (95°F [35°C]) into cold mash will shock the yeast.**

By following this procedure, the yeast is in an optimal condition and fermentation can begin quickly. In addition, unwanted microorganisms are quickly suppressed.

What are Enzymes?
(***Also Called Biocatalysts***)

Addition of Enzymes

Enzyme Treatment of Fruit Mashes

Fruit consists of countless cells which are held together by pectin, a cementing substance. Pome fruits, in particular, contain a large amount of pectin, consequently their mashes are often very viscous.

Rowanberry mash: (left) without enzyme; (right) treated with enzyme—more liquid.

During fermentation the pectin slowly breaks down and the mash becomes thinner. As the sugar required for fermentation is found in the cells, a quicker breakdown of pectin is extremely desirable, as this causes the mash to thin more quickly. The cell tissue breaks down in the process and fermentation proceeds more rapidly. Pectin enzyme compounds (pectolytic enzyme), which quickly break down the pectin in the fruit (depending on temperature), are now commercially available.

WHAT ARE ENZYMES? (*ALSO CALLED BIOCATALYSTS*)

Enzymes are active substances which affect chemical processes without being consumed. The entire metabolic process in humans, animals, and plants is essentially based on the effects of enzymes. In most cases an enzyme causes one very specific reaction. Several enzymes are required for complicated metabolic processes; for example, 12 different enzymes are needed for alcoholic fermentation.

Pectin Enzyme

Among the many enzymes are those which break down pectin so that the cell structure can disintegrate. Yeast probably produces these enzymes, too, but in limited quantities, so that pectin breakdown takes place very slowly. By adding enzymes that break down pectin, pectin is removed in a few hours or days, depending on temperature. Although optimal effectiveness is achieved at 104-122°F (40-50°C), the enzyme's effect is still satisfactory at lower temperatures (64.4-68°F [18-20°C]). Effectiveness decreases rapidly at lower temperatures and below 50°F (10°C) is almost non-existent. Numerous compounds are commercially available, such as Pektinex, Ultra SP-L, Siha-Brennereienzym SK Plus, etc. On each enzyme bottle label there are precise instructions for usage and dosing information for the various types of fruit. Enzyme compounds are available in liquid and granular forms.

Enzymes make mashes more liquid.

Good distribution of the enzyme in the mash is achieved by introducing the enzyme—which is thinned with water, mash, or juice—into the mash mill in portions with the fruit.

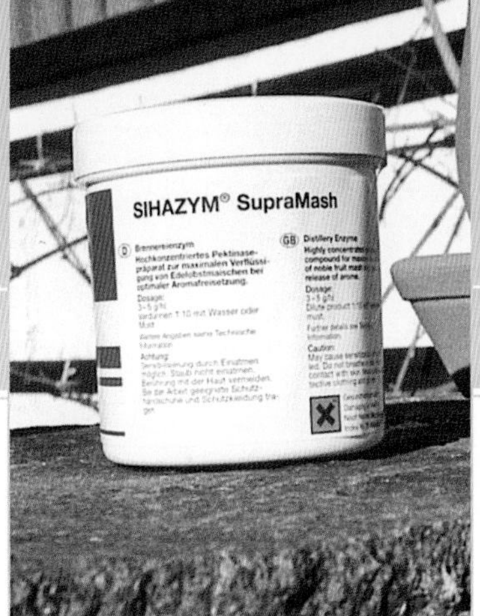

Granular enzyme.

ADDITION OF ENZYME

If the addition of enzyme is required, the thinned enzyme compound and the swollen yeast are alternately added via the mash mill during mashing or stirred into the mash. The next day stir thoroughly once more.

The amount used differs based on the product and type of fruit. Use as per the instructions accompanying the product.

The enzyme can also be mixed with the yeast. In case of acidification, the enzyme can be added with the yeast before or after (based on the manufacturer's recommendation).

> Prior acidification is more beneficial for the yeast, as it can be damaged if acidification occurs later.
>
> If acidification takes place after addition of the enzyme (several hours later), the enzyme works somewhat faster, however the enzyme effect is still satisfactory to pH 3.

Enzyme-treated mashes are so thin that they can easily be distilled without the addition of water.

Enzyme compounds are very concentrated, therefore the application rate is between 3 and 30 ml (g)/100 l, depending on compound and raw material.

Study the manufacturer's instructions before using enzymes.

Advantages of enzyme treatment, which is particularly effective with pome fruit mashes:

- rapid liquefaction of the mash
- better pumpability
- faster and more complete fermentation
- reduced foam formation
- better heat transmission during distillate because of thinness
- easier stirring of various mash treatment materials

Enzyme treatment results in good mash preparation and better fermentation; it only appears to result in improved alcohol yield.

The use of enzymes with stone fruits causes the stones to separate from the flesh more quickly and sink to the bottom; the use of enzymes is especially recommended with firm-fleshed fruits.

The use of enzymes results in a minimal increase in alcohol yield at best. What appears to be a higher yield is often caused by the good preparation of the mash and resulting improved fermentation. The use of enzymes also produces no detectable effects on the flavor of the finished distillate.

One-year shelf life in refrigerator.

Shelf Life

If kept in a refrigerator, the enzyme compounds will retain their full effectiveness for a year. At room temperature, effectiveness decreases by 1 to 2% per month. If possible, one should only buy a quantity of enzyme that can be used in one season. Enzyme thinned with water is only stable for a few hours, therefore only thin as much enzyme as can be used in one to two hours. In rare cases enzymes can cause allergies, therefore wear rubber gloves as a precaution or avoid handling the enzyme with bare hands.

pH Value

pH Measurement

Acid Treatment
(*Fermentation with Acid Protection*)

Acidification

Necessary with:
- acid-poor raw materials
- unhygienic processing
- extended storage of fermented mash

pH VALUE

The pH value is the scale for measuring the acidic or alkaline character of a water-based solution. A neutral solution has a pH value of 7. From pH 7 to 14 the solution becomes increasingly alkaline, and from pH 7 to 0 increasingly acidic. The term pH (*pondus hydrogenii*) means the weight of the hydrogen ions in a water solution.

pH MEASUREMENT

1 There are dyes that change color based on the pH value. The cheapest and easiest way to determine pH value is to use indicator paper or indicator strips. For fruit mashes the measurement range should lie between pH 2.5 and 4.5. Merck's indicator test strip No. 9541 is recommended for fruit mashes, but of course other products will do the job just as well.

Indicator paper and strips can only be used once and should be stored in a dry place. Accurate readings should be possible in increments of 0.2 pH. Colorful liquids cannot be measured as the change in test strip or paper color will not be recognizable.

2 pH values can also be measured with an electric pH meter. Measurements can be obtained quickly and this method is ideal for colorful mashes such as elderberry and cherry.

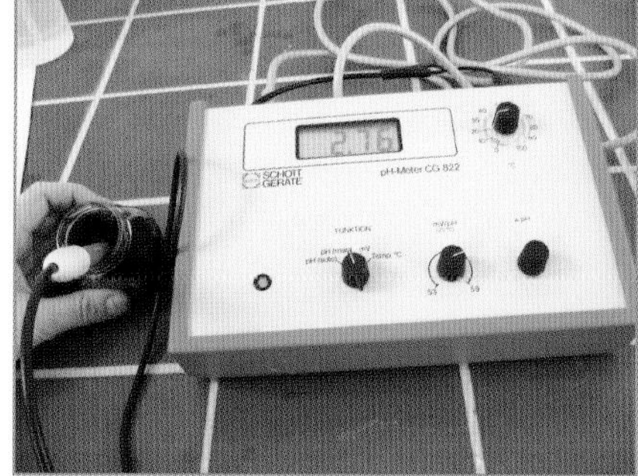

Electric pH meters must always be recalibrated to ensure accurate readings. Only buy a pH meter that allows the user to occasionally recalibrate the instrument!

pH Values of Known Liquids		
	pH	Reaction
Hydrochloric acid	0	extremely acidic
Sulfuric acid	1.2	highly acidic
Tartaric acid	2.2	medium acidity
Vinegar	3.1	weak acidity
Wine, fruit mashes	3.0-3.8	weak acidity
Apple mash, fermented *(table fruit)*	3.5-4.2	weak acidity
Apple mash, fermented *(must fruit)*	3.0-3.5	weak acidity
Pear mash, fermented *(table fruit)*	3.7-4.0	weak acidity
Pear mash, fermented *(must fruit)*	3.4-3.8	weak acidity
Beer	4.0-5.0	very weak acidity
Pure water	7.0	neutral
Sea water	8.3	weak alkalinity
Soda solution (0.5%)	11.3	medium alkalinity
Lime water, saturated	12.3	highly alkaline
Caustic soda	14.0	extremely alkaline

ACID TREATMENT (*FERMENTATION WITH ACID PROTECTION*)

Only carry out with required pH measurements!

Harmful microorganisms can multiply more rapidly in acid-poor mashes, but their development can be checked through the addition of acid, resulting in a cleaner, purer fermentation. The addition of acid is therefore highly recommended for acid-poor fruits like golden delicious apples, raspberries, elderberries, apricots, peaches, etc.

Especially important with acid-poor fruits and storage of fermented mashes.

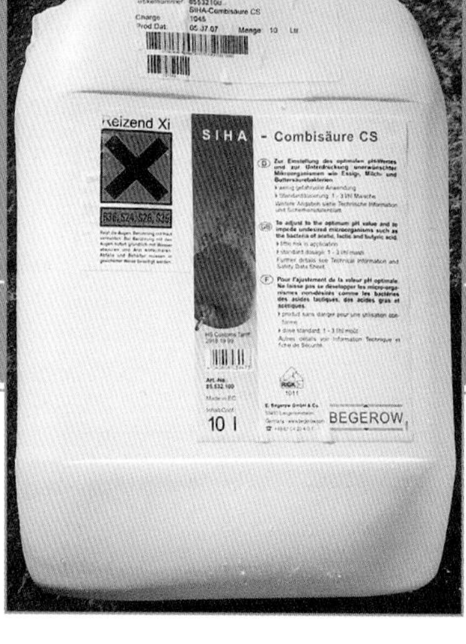

Combisäure acid treatment.

If the fruit is clean and healthy and the mash will be distilled as soon as fermentation is completed, a mash pH value of 3.0-3.2 will suffice. At this pH level there is still a sufficient enzyme effect. If a longer storage of the mash is required, acid can be added after the completion of fermentation to achieve a pH value of about 2.8.

Which Acids Are Used?

Various acid combinations are commercially available. They mainly contain lactic acid, phosphoric acid, or malic acid. They are known under the brand names Combisäure CS, MS-Säure, etc.

The rate of application is always indicated on the package and is generally 1 to 2 liters per 150–300 g/hl. The higher value is intended for use with acid-poor fruits like Williams Christ pears, elderberries, raspberries, apricots, etc. By measuring the pH value, one can easily determine the appropriate quantity. Phosphoric acid also has the advantage of serving as yeast nourishment. The addition of phosphoric acid is banned in Germany, however.

Acidification is also possible with sulfuric acid. For small distillers the use of acid combinations is simpler and is therefore recommended.

Acid Can Be Added in Two Ways

- Yeast and enzyme are first added through the mill or by stirring into the mash. Mix thoroughly one or two times more, and after several hours carefully mix in the acid combination (*according to the instructions and pH value*).
- Acidify first, mix well, and then add yeast and enzyme. Always set the pH level at 3.0-3.2.

Can One Forego Acidification?

Many small distillers want nothing to do with it. With painstaking cleanliness, an optimally prepared yeast mixture, a fermentation vessel sealed with an airlock, and proper fermentation temperature, the mash should be distilled as fermentation is ending or has ended. In this case one can often forego acidification.

Acidification is recommended if the mash has to be left standing for longer periods.

When Is the Addition of Acid Beneficial?

When processing acid-poor raw materials like Williams Christ pears, cherries, plums, peaches, elderberries, cornelian, or bird cherries, as well as poor raw material and windfall.

pH meter.

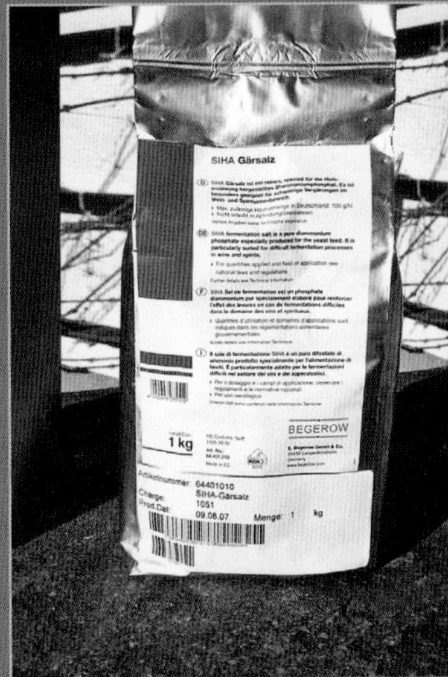

Yeast salt.

Yeast Salts

For rapid multiplication, yeast needs nitrogen and phosphorous compounds as well as vitamins (*especially Vitamin B1*).
These substances are lacking in some fruits, especially blueberries, elderberries, Rowan berries, sloes, and rose hips. They may also be present in inadequate quantities in pome fruits rich in tannin, such as must pears. The absence of these yeast nutrients can result in slow fermentation and in extreme cases stoppage of fermentation.

Application Rate

For these fruits, the application rate is 30-40g per hl of mash. In distilling shops these materials are sold as yeast salt, fermenting salt, etc. They should be used according to directions.

If fermentation problems arise with other types of fruit despite the addition of yeast and the correct fermentation temperature, the addition of half the indicated quantity of yeast salt can solve the problem. Ammonium sulfate and ammonium dihydrogen phosphate can also be used as yeast food, although procuring these materials is rather difficult.

The addition of yeast salt is permitted in Austria, but is banned in some other countries. Always follow the local ordinances.

Iodine solution for iodine test—detects presence of starch.

Amylase

Amylase are enzymes that break starches down into sugar. If pome fruits are not properly ripened, starches may be present. The presence of starch can be detected quickly with an iodine test.

Iodine Test

One puts a few drops of iodine on the fruit flesh. If a blue color appears, starch is present and the fruit is not completely ripe. If fruit still contains starch when mashed (iodine test), the addition of amylase can break down the starch into sugar. Follow instructions for use.

Iodine solution for iodine test—detects presence of starch.

It must be emphasized that the distilling monopoly expressly forbids home and commercial distillers from adding sugar, fruit juice, or wine.

Other Additives

Extract Contents of Distilled and Undistilled Mashes

	Extract Content Undistilled		Extract Content Distilled	
Type of Fruit	Saccharometer %mas (% extract)	Must Scale °Must Weight	Saccharometer %mas (% extract)	Must Scale °Must Weight
Apples*	12-17	48-68	1-3	4-12
Golden Delicious	12-19	48-76	0-2	0-8
Pears	10-17	40-68	2-4	8-16
Williams Christ Pears	10-14	40-56	2-4	8-16
Quinces	10-14	40-56	3-4	12-16
Cherries	14-30	56-120	4-9	16-36
Sour Cherries*	12-16	48-64	2-4	8-16
Plums	10-25	40-100	4-6	16-24
Plums*	10-15	40-60	2-3	8-12
Mirabelles	16-22	64-88	2-5	8-20
Raspberries*	8-10	32-40	1-2	4-8
Elderberries*	8-11	32-44	3-5	12-20
Rowan berries	15-25	60-100	9-18	36-72
Rowan berries, sweet	15-18	60-72	7-8	28-32

according to Peiper et al 1993

Mashing

MASH ADDITIVES

- **Yeast:** absolutely necessary for a clean, smooth fermentation, preferably cold yeast to ensure a good fermentation process even at lower temperatures.
- **Enzyme:** to thin viscous mashes.
- **Acid:** added to suppress harmful microorganisms when low-acid raw materials are used or with careless preparation.
- **Yeast Nutrients:** occasionally needed to improve nourishment of the yeast.
- **Amylase:** to convert starch into sugar.

Mashing = preparing the raw materials for fermentation.

Mashing places the raw materials for distillation in a fermentable condition.

Sweet fruits and roots store their fructose and dextrose in the cells. The yeast must then turn this sugar into alcohol (*see Fermentation*). It is therefore necessary that the cells be partly ruptured in order to release the fructose and dextrose.

Mash preparation and addition of the necessary additives.

Photo 1: Fruit in the water bath in front of the ratz mill.
Photo 2: Rinsing off of dirty water.
Photo 3: Measuring enzyme additive.
Photo 4: Enzyme thinned in water is added to the mash. Mixing takes place in the mash pump.
Photo 5: Adding yeast salt.

Further breakdown of the cells is brought about by the yeast itself during fermentation. Pure selected yeast is of critical importance for an optimal fermentation process.

It is important that the selected yeast be started properly.

Optimal activation can only take place in a 1:1 juice/water or mash/water mixture at 95°F (35°C). Lowering the yeast mixture's temperature to that of the mash must take place slowly. Placing it into the cold (64.4°F [18°C]) mash will shock the yeast and it can become partially deactivated.

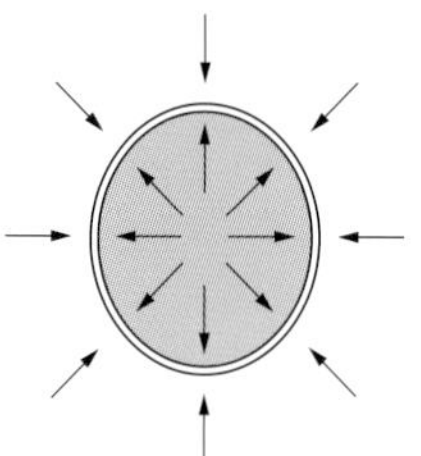
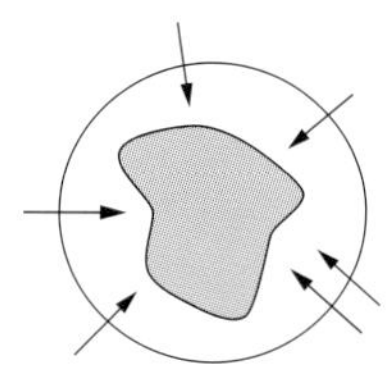
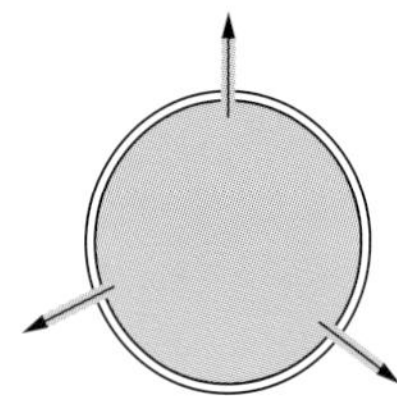

Methods of rehydrating dry pure selected yeast in various media (*arrows indicate the pressure affecting the yeast cells*).

Suitable mash mills are available with which to crush the various types of raw materials.

MASH MILLS

When dealing with large quantities of fruit, it pays to procure a suitable mash mill. Selection depends on the amount of fruit to be processed and the price. Larger pieces often pass through the mill and one must take care to ensure that these are fully fermented during the fermentation process.

Scraper mill, right—opened with wooden rams and scraper roller.

Scraper Mill

A scraper mill has a wooden roller with straight-edge or serrated metal blades. A wooden ram pushes the fruit against the roller. Somewhat larger pieces often pass through the mill, and care must be taken during fermentation to ensure that these pieces are also completely fermented. Despite this, the scraper mill is very good for smaller quantities of fruit.

They are suitable for pome fruits, for they function in a way that leaves the cores intact.

Centrifugal Mill (*Ratz Mill*)

A high-performance mill very well suited to processing large quantities of fruit. It comes with different graters for the various types of fruit. This mill produces a fine, consistent mash without pureeing the fruit. It is suitable for pome and stone fruits and berries and spares the stones and cores.

Stone or Star Roller Mill

These mills are hardly made any more. Grab hooks crush the fruit, which is

Barrel masher.

then crushed. The rollers are adjustable, making it possible to process various kinds of fruit. Crushing of the fruit is satisfactory, so that one can comfortably continue using these mills.

Centrifugal mill.

Feed Masher

The feed masher turns the fruit into a fine mush, consequently it can only be used for pome fruits and berries. The stones in stone fruits would be crushed and too much poisonous hydrogen cyanide would be produced during fermentation. In addition, the cores of apples and pears should not be crushed, as they transmit an unpleasant taste to the distillate.

Definitely remove rotten fruit.

FRUIT SELECTION AND PREPARATION

Proper fruit selection is crucial for a clean, smooth fermentation and a flawless distillate.

It must be healthy, fully ripe, clean, and free of foreign odors. Rotten, wrinkled, or damaged fruit must be removed. Also, no green fruit should be used (*it has little flavor or aroma*).

Preparation of Raw Materials

Dirty fruit must be washed and then rinsed to ensure that all dirty water is removed from the fruit. Even seemingly clean fruit (*one cannot see microorganisms*) should be spray washed. Examination of cherries has shown that significantly fewer microorganisms (*mildew, vinegar bacteria, Kahm yeast, etc.*) are present on washed cherries.

Mash Temperature

This stage of raw materials preparation plays a very important part in determining the quality of the finished brandy.

For a quick start to fermentation, fruit should be at mash temperature.

Mash temperature is crucial for quick fermentation. It is most simple when the fruit is pre-warmed in the sun or in a warm space. Warming also promotes post-ripening. The mash temperature should be in the region of 64.4°F (18°C). Harvesting fruit in the morning and mashing it immediately is a mistake. The mash is then too cold and the commencement of fermentation is delayed or fermentation can become stuck (*no alcohol is formed*). Fruit temperature 64.4-68°F (18-20° C).

Apples and Pears

Crush apples and pears in a suitable mash mill. Coarse crushing does not rupture the cells sufficiently, consequently not all of the sugar will be fermented. This can result in severely reduced alcohol yield.

> **If a single-wall vessel is used, the mash should be somewhat coarser (*danger of catching fire*).**

The current trend in fruit brandy making is the production of single-variety brandies. Each variety transmits its own aroma to the brandy. Preferred varieties are: Williams Christ pears, Boskoop, Jonagold, Elstar, Gravenstein, etc.

For the small commercial distiller, it is difficult to procure sufficient quantities of a specific variety of fruit. If quantities are too small, the harsh brandy can be kept for the following year. Brandies made of mixed varieties continue to be popular, however.

If a column still is used, enough fruit to fill the vessel once is sufficient, as it is only run once.

Warning! Broken stones will result in prussic acid in the distillate.

Stone Fruits

Damsons and plums are crushed, however their stones should not be damaged.

There are two possibilities for subsequent processing:

- The entire fruit, which consists of the stone and flesh, can be mashed, after which both are present in the distillate.
- The stones can be removed by hand or machine prior to mashing and just the flesh is mashed. In this way only the fruit aroma is present in the distillate. Finally, up to 1/3 of the stones can be added for fermentation and then removed prior to distillation. Variations of this are also possible.

Peaches should be pitted. Only after the stones have been removed can peaches be crushed and treated with enzymes. After the stones have been removed, the mash should be decanted using a grate. Peach stones give the distillate a bitter taste.

Mirabelle plums have large stones. Once again the stone should not be damaged and only a few or even none of the stones should be present during distillation.

Cherries should be mashed without the stones, otherwise the distillate has a tart, strange taste.

Mash cherries without stems—otherwise the distillate will have a bitter taste.

Acid should be added prior to fermentation.

Before mixing stone fruits, one should first consider their different alcohol yields. In Austria the alcohol tax is always calculated based on the fruit with the highest alcohol yield. Check your local tax code and relevant regulations before distilling fruit brandy or making any other type of alcoholic beverages.

Berries

Remove tops, stems, and leaves, crush, add pure selected yeast. If the mash is too viscous, add enzymes and perhaps yeast nutrient. When fermentation is ending or has ended, carefully distill.

Observe the proper harvesting time, this is particularly important for elderberries.

Elderberries

Use only fully ripened berries. The stems absolutely must be removed to prevent undesirable substances from contaminating the distillate. The berries can be removed from the twigs by rubbing them over a screen. The mesh size must be at least twice as large as the diameter of the greatest berry (*see Rowan berry photo*). For more information see "Special Brandies" (pg. 129).

Rowan Berries

Here again one should only use fully ripened berries with the stems removed. Place a piece of mesh (such as rabbit wire) in a frame, lay the entire thing over a tub and strip off the berries through the screen. The berries themselves should then be run through a mash mill. For more information see "Special Brandies" (pg. 125).

Winnowing Rowan berries over a wire screen.

A press as used in winemaking can also be used to separate the berries from the tops. They are less effective, however.

Grapes

Best suited are the aromatic grapes, such as Muskat or Traminer, which produce a distillate with sufficient aroma. Press the grapes (*remove stems*), add the yeast and ferment at a moderate temperature (64.4°F [18°C]).

Juniper Berries

Fresh juniper berries are seldom distilled and are of little importance. Only dried berries are processed. The crushed berries are placed in double the normal amount of water. Fermentation is somewhat difficult and the addition of yeast nutrient is necessary.

A pleasant-tasting brandy is obtained if apple or pear mash is added. This also results in problem-free fermentation. For more information see "Special Brandies" (pg. 125).

Add roots to an apple or pear mash.

Roots

Commercial distilleries rarely mash and distill roots alone. An apple or pear mash is added to the cleaned and well-processed roots. For more information see "Special Brandies" (pg. 125).

It is necessary to add water to some raw materials.

ADDING WATER

It is widely believed that warm water must always be added to the mash. Often the amount of water added is equal to 30% of the mash. If one asks for a reason, the answer is that one should warm up the mash with warm water in order to make it thin enough for fermentation.

As stressed in the chapter on mashing, the fruit should be warmed (64.4-68°F [18-20°C]). In principle, the addition of water is not necessary for fermentation. Water should only be added to very dry mashes (such as Rowan berries) in which hollow cavities may form. Even then, the water added should only be sufficient to fill the hollow cavities. In this case, without the addition of water, mold may form or the mash may become overheated.

The addition of water increases the overall volume, which may be subject to tax. Check your local tax code and regulations.

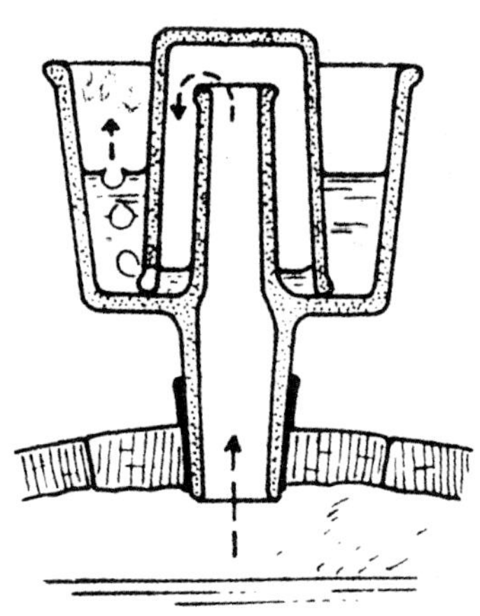

Cross-section of an airlock.

FILLING THE FERMENTATION VESSEL

The milled or crushed raw materials are placed in a clean fermentation vessel. The necessary additives (*yeast, enzyme, acid, and yeast nutrient*) are either added through the mill or are stirred in at this point. Fill the container to the 9/10ths mark, seal well, and fit an airlock with a sealing liquid (water, sulfurous acid). The carbon dioxide must only be able to escape through the airlock so that the fermentation process can be well monitored. The fermentation vessel should be filled all at once, in order to guarantee clean, pure fermentation.

Stirring the Mash

If the additives (*yeast, enzyme*) have been well mixed and the mash is thin enough, there is no need to stir any further. To better distribute the additives, the mash can be stirred one or two times or the skin can be pierced. Any handling causes air to enter the mash and the protective carbon dioxide layer is destroyed.

The yeast needs no additional oxygen, whereas the oxygen-dependent microorganisms do. The surface of the mash should be rather brown. If this is stirred in, fresh mash comes to the surface and in turn becomes brown. In the event of a thick skin buildup and the danger of drying out (*Rowan berries, elderberries, etc.)*, a possible remedy is to insert a screen cover, which holds the mash under the liquid.

If the mash foams heavily during fermentation, an anti-foaming agent can be added (*amount as per directions for use*). Fermentation in open containers is not recommended as it invariably leads to fermentation problems.

Progress of fermentation can be followed by observing the airlock.

Provided there are no fermentation interruptions, the vessels remain sealed until fermentation is complete.

Room temperature should be at least 59°F (15°C) to ensure rapid fermentation, although 64.4-68°F (18-20°C) is better. Smaller vessels require a higher room temperature as they cool off more rapidly.

Various types of airlock.

Anti-foaming agent.

FERMENTATION DURATION

This is two weeks in the best case, but it can take six weeks or more (*Rowan berries, for example*).

After enzyme treatment, fermentation of the mash can be complete after 14 days. This depends on the fermenting temperature and the fineness of the mash as well as the type of fruit.

Unfortunately, there is no simple and reliable method of determining when fermentation has ended. Practitioners say that the mash has completed fermentation when the skin sinks to the bottom or when a match burns just above the surface of the mash. Unfortunately this is not true, for it only proves that the mash is no longer fermenting. The mash may be completely fermented, but fermentation may only have become interrupted.

If fermentation is interrupted, a fermentation test is necessary.

Determining the End of Fermentation

If the fermentation process has been observed at the airlock (*primary, secondary, and final fermentation*), one can say relatively accurately when fermentation has ended. If the fermentation process has been irregular or interrupted, a fermentation test can confirm the end of fermentation. Unfermented mashes still contain fermentable sugar.

Obtaining mash juice for extract measurement.

Fermentation Test

Take a piece of cheese cloth, place some mash in it and allow the liquid to flow off. The mash is then squeezed and the juice collected for extract testing (*see "Extract Testing," pg. 16*). If fermentation is complete, all of the sugar in the bits of mash has been fermented. As previously described, measurements of sugar content obtained with a saccharometer also include the substances dissolved in the juice. The readings can be compared to the empirical values for unfermented substances (*see table on pg. 29*).

If sugar remains in the mash the alcohol yield is reduced.

Remaining Sugar

If the saccharometer reading is higher than the values given in the table, the most likely culprit is remaining sugar. In this case one pours the juice into a bottle, adds a little baker's or dry yeast, seals the bottle with a cotton ball and lets it sit at 64.4-68°F (18-20°C). After three or four days, test again. If the reading remains the same, it can be assumed that the mash is fermented. If the reading is lower, sugar was still present, which means that the mash is not yet completely fermented. One must therefore put off distillation.

Example of Fermentation Test (Apple)

See pg. 26 for Extract measurement.

Extract content before fermentation test	3.7 %mas
Extract content after fermentation test	2.5 %mas
Remaining fermentable sugar	1.2 %mas

In this case fermentation is not complete.

Example

The juice of an apple mash has 4 %mas extract, which means that it is not fermented (*the figure for apples in the table below is 1-3 %mas extract*).

For enzyme-treated mashes, juice strained through a cloth or filter is tested. The mash particles have disintegrated to the point that they have a mushy consistency and cannot be pressed out any further, which in this case is not necessary. Shake the juice once more before testing with a saccharometer, so that any remaining carbon dioxide can escape, as the carbon dioxide's buoyancy could result in a false reading.

If one has several containers of the same mash, it is sufficient to conduct the fermentation test on the contents of just one. The extract content after the fermentation test (2.5 %mas in the example) is valid for all of the containers with the same mash in the same room.

Another way of measuring sugar is the Clinitest Method (color test). One uses a complete testing kit with measuring tubes, color scale, and tablets.

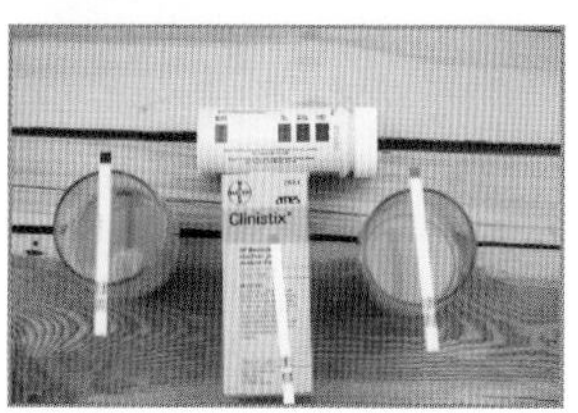

Clini-Test and Clinistix.

A further possibility is to use Clinistix. These are strips used to test for urinary sugar. They indicate whether fruit sugar is present as glucose and fructose. Both types of sugar ferment quite quickly, therefore if no glucose is present it is safe to assume that the fructose has also been fermented. Color tests for detecting sugar can only be used with colorless to slightly tinted liquids.

The degree of fermentation of Rowan berries is approximately 7 %mas extract *(saccharometer)* or 28° Öchsle. These values vary significantly and depend on the amount of water added to the mash, the ripeness of the fruit, and whether wild or cultivated Rowan berries are used. In any case, a fermentation test should be carried out (see pg. 66).

Degrees of Fermentation

(apparent extract of fermented fruit mashes and fruit musts)

Material	Saccharometer (from PLATO) (%mas)	Must Weight (Temp = 68°F) (Must Weight)	Sources
Apple	1-3	4-12	WINDISCH/RÜDIGER/ SCHWARZ/MALSCH (1965)
Table Apples (11 varieties)	0.2-1.9	~1-7.5	RÖHRIG/PIEPER (1979)
Single-Variety Table Apples			
James Grieve	0.6-1.4	~2.5-5.5	RÖHRIG/PIEPER (1979)
Gravenstein	0.2-1.8	~1-7	RÖHRIG/PIEPER (1979)
Goldparmäne	0.2-1.5	~1-5	RÖHRIG/PIEPER (1982-83)[1]
Cox	0.1-1.5	~0.5-6	RÖHRIG/PIEPER (1982-83)[1] PIEPER/BÜCHMÜLLER (1978)[1]
Jonathan	0.5-1.9	~2-7.5	RÖHRIG/PIEPER (1982-83)[1]
Boskoop	0.4-1.9	~1.5-7.5	RÖHRIG/PIEPER (1982-83)[1]
Golden Delicious	0.1-1.8	~0.5-7	RÖHRIG/PIEPER (1982-83)[1] PIEPER/BÜCHMÜLLER (1978)[1]
Red Delicious	0.3-0.8	~1-3	RÖHRIG/PIEPER (1982-83)[1]
McIntosh	0.5-0.6	~2-2.5	RÖHRIG/PIEPER (1982-83)[1]
Jonagold	0.3-1.1	~1-4.5	RÖHRIG/PIEPER (1982-83)[1]
Pears	1.5-4	6-16	WINDISCH/RÜDIGER/ SCHWARZ/MALSCH (1965)
Table Pears (11 varieties)	0.7-3.6	3-14.5	RÖHRIG/PIEPER (1982-83)
Williams Christ Pears	1.7-4	7-16	WINDISCH/RÜDIGER/ SCHWARZ/MALSCH (1965)
Must Pears (Jaköble)	2.2	8.8	RÖHRIG/PIEPER (1979)
	3-5	12-20	WINDISCH/RÜDIGER/ SCHWARZ/MALSCH (1965)
Sour Cherries (14 varieties)	2-4	8-16	PIEPER/GRAF (1985)

Degrees of Fermentation

(apparent extract of fermented fruit mashes and fruit musts)

Material	Saccharometer (from PLATO) (%mas)	Must Weight (Temp = 68°F) (Must Weight)	Sources
Damsons	4-5	16-20	WINDISCH/RÜDIGER/ SCHWARZ/MALSCH (1965)
Plums	2-3	8-12	WINDISCH/RÜDIGER/ SCHWARZ/MALSCH (1965)
Mirabelle Plums	2-4	8-16	WINDISCH/RÜDIGER/ SCHWARZ/MALSCH (1965)
Raspberries, Blackberries	1-2	4-8	WINDISCH/RÜDIGER/ SCHWARZ/MALSCH (1965)
Blueberries	3-5	12-20	WINDISCH/RÜDIGER/ SCHWARZ/MALSCH (1965)
Jerusalem Artichoke	1	4	WINDISCH/RÜDIGER/ SCHWARZ/MALSCH (1965)
Must (Must Pears 7 Varieties)	0.2-2.6	0-10.4	RÖHRIG/PIEPER (1979)

[1]Taking into account the results of ongoing research from 1975 to 1980 by the Dept. of Fermentation Technology at the University of Hohenheim using fruit from the Bodensee region, always from the same location.

INTERRUPTIONS IN THE FERMENTATION PROCESS

Every interruption in the fermentation process affects alcohol yield and aroma.

It often happens that the fermentation process is interrupted, which means that the yeast stops multiplying and sugar ceases to be converted into alcohol. In most cases the cause is a fermentation temperature that is too low. If the fruit temperature is 64.4-68°F (18-20°C) when mashed and the fermentation vessels are in a sufficiently warm room, the mash temperature can never drop low enough to halt yeast reproduction. If the temperature really has fallen too low, the mash must be warmed. To do this, part of the mash is removed from the vessel and heated to a maximum of 113°F (45°C) (the yeast will die at higher temperatures). One can check with the responsible government agency to find out whether the mash can be heated in the still. If mash must be heated, that is the best way. The heated mash is then stirred into the cold mash. This is done until the mash temperature reaches a minimum of 64.4°F (18°C). In addition, some cold yeast and yeast nutrient can be added to the mash.

Lack of nitrogen for the yeast is seldom encountered in small commercial distilleries; it can, however, occur with the following types of fruit: blueberries,

Healthy mash (apple).

Rowan berries, rosehip, juniper berries, and sloes. If problems are encountered with these mashes, after mashing add 1.4oz (40g) of yeast salt dissolved in water per hectoliter.

Too much tannin can also hamper fermentation. This can be countered by adding mash low in fermentation substances and some water.

Mixing of Mashes

Fermented mashes can be mixed at any time (*pome fruit to pome fruit, cherries to cherries, etc.*). One may have to consider the tax differences, however

Mash without acid protection.

MASH HANDLING AFTER FERMENTATION

In order to obtain quality fruit brandies, fruit mashes should be made ready for distillation as soon as fermentation abates or ends. Only thus are optimal aroma yield and good quality possible.

If one knows at the time of mashing that the mash will be stored longer than 3-4 weeks, it should definitely be fermented with acid protection (see pg. 52).

When fermentation has ended, seal the fermentation vessel air tight and allow it to cool. Do not open the vessel, which risks destroying the carbon dioxide layer that shields the mash from oxygen.

Storage of Mashes that Were Fermented without Acid Protection

- For short-term storage of 3-4 weeks after fermentation has ended, seal the fermentation vessels air tight and store them in a cool place. Once fermentation is nearing an end, do not open the vessels again to prevent oxygen from entering. When the vessels are opened, and there is no layer of mold on the mash and no vinegar smell is noticeable, then the airlock functioned correctly.
- For storage of more than 3-4 weeks, when fermentation tapers off, acid should be added (see pg. 52) to achieve a pH of 2.8-3. Afterwards the mash container must be again sealed air tight and placed in the coolest possible place. Only thus can unwanted changes in the mash, for the most part, be avoided.

Acid is added as fermentation is waning and not after it is complete so that some more carbon dioxide can form, which forces out the oxygen.

Mash with kahm yeast.

Filling the fermentation vessels after fermentation is somewhat problematic. This allows oxygen to enter the mash, and Kahm yeast, vinegar bacteria, and other harmful microorganisms may develop.

Proper storage of damson mash for 5-6 months is claimed to produce a brandy with special qualities. There are also varieties of cherry that benefit from a mash storage of two to three months.

Wooden containers are poorly suited for storing mash for longer periods (entry of oxygen, evaporation). For lengthier storage of mash one should use only airtight plastic or stainless steel containers.

WHEN TO DISTILL

Timing of distillation is a critical factor in the quality of the distillate.

Aroma is a critical element of fruit brandies. The greatest aroma yield occurs when fermentation is winding down or has ended. Fermentation of fruits with a delicate aroma, such as Williams Christ pears, raspberries, strawberries, but also apples, should be aborted as fermentation is winding down. Storage of fermentation mashes usually leads to a loss of aroma and quality. One should, if possible, schedule mashing so that mash storage is not necessary. If time is a factor, the mash should at least be turned into harsh brandy.

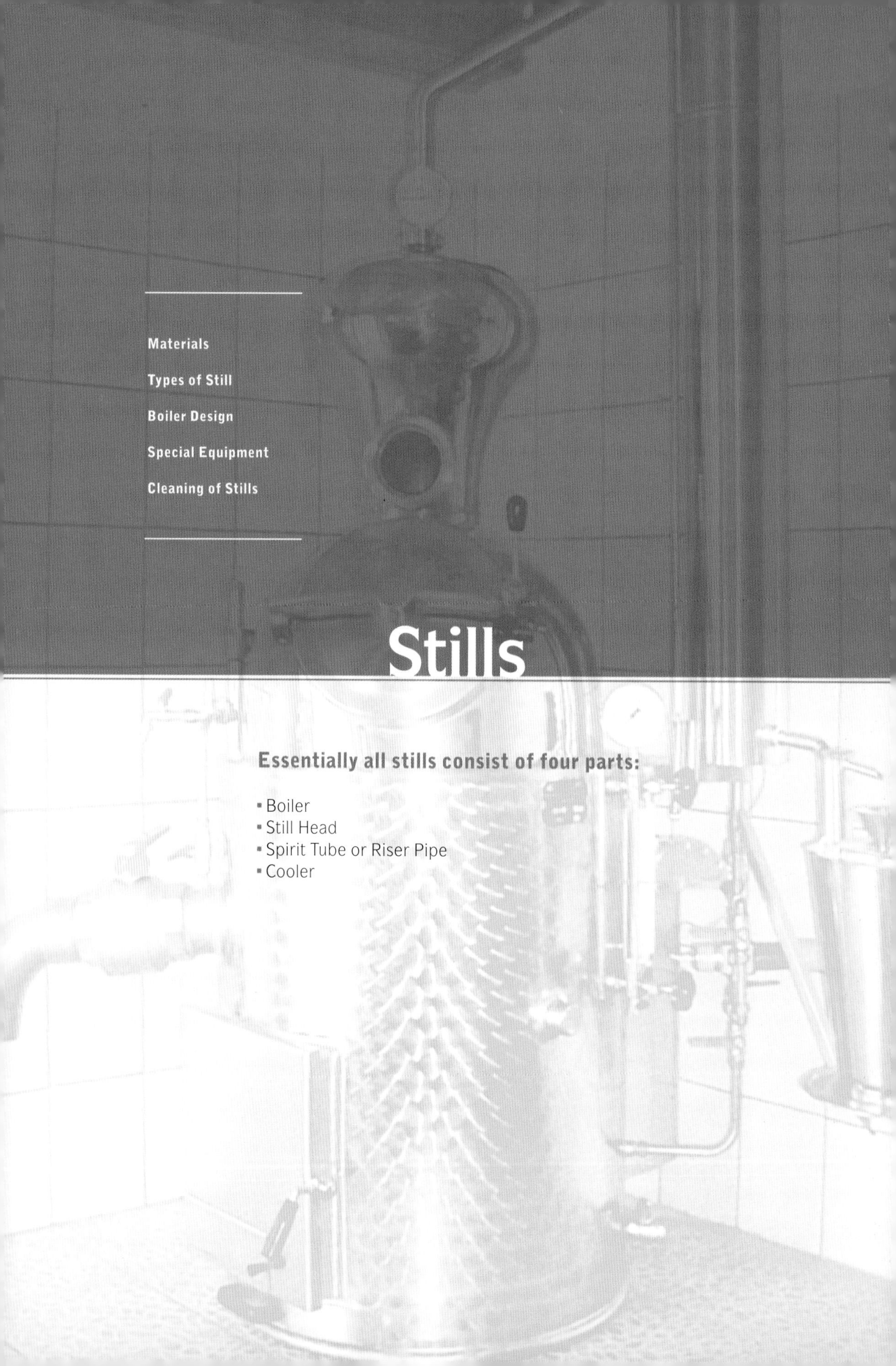

Materials

Types of Still

Boiler Design

Special Equipment

Cleaning of Stills

Stills

Essentially all stills consist of four parts:

- Boiler
- Still Head
- Spirit Tube or Riser Pipe
- Cooler

MATERIALS

Nowadays copper is the only material considered for use. Stainless steel has not stood the test, except for cooling lines and piping, as it does not patine like copper. Copper also absorbs various substances (hydrogen sulfide) which would otherwise find their way into the distillate. Stainless steel stills are therefore unsuited to the production of quality brandy.

Each part of the still has an important role to play during distillation and it is important that the distiller be aware of this.

Boiler

The boiler is used to heat the mash so that the volatile substances can evaporate. Copper has outstanding heat-conducting properties. This is important for conserving fuel as well as for good heat distribution and heat transfer to the mash.

Head

Atop the boiler is the so-called head, which comes in many different shapes. All that matters is that the head forms a sufficiently large space above the boiler. This space serves as a collection area for the vapor that forms. The head plays a particularly important role as a pre-cooler. Cooling results from its large surface

Various still head designs.

area and the excellent conductivity of the material (copper). First the substances with the higher boiling points—in our case water and the higher alcohols—liquefy on the inner surface of the head. Substances with a higher boiling point than potable alcohol in part run back down the inside of the head into the mash. In case of foaming liquid, as a last measure one can place a cold, wet cloth on the head. This causes the foam to cool and collapse into itself. If the mash foams, an anti-foaming agent can be added.

The head leads into the spirit tube or riser pipe.

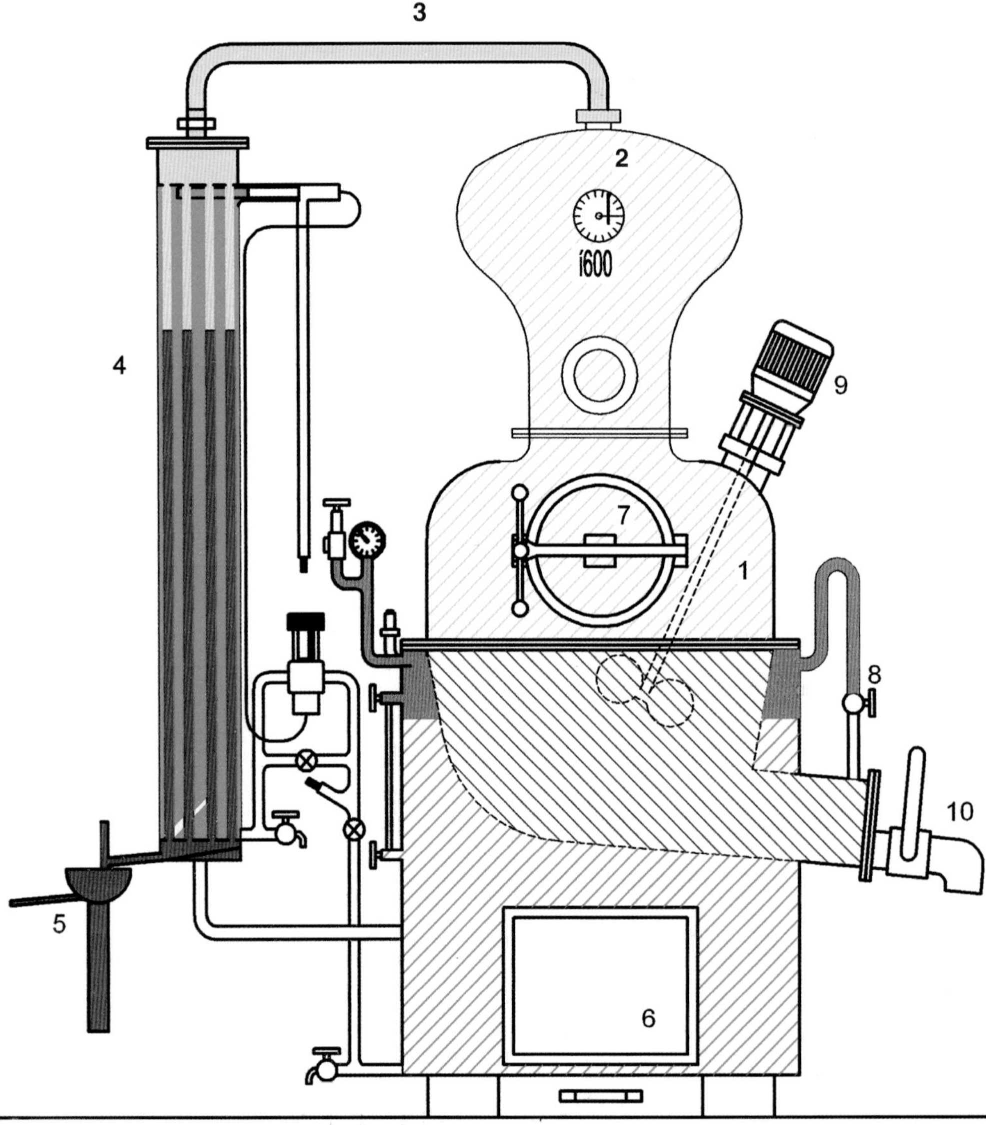

Water Bath Still with Still Head and Agitator, Holstein Company

1. Boiler
2. Head
3. Riser pipe
4. Cooler
5. Sight box
6. Water bath with fire box
7. Filler opening
8. Steam line
9. Agitator
10. Mash drain

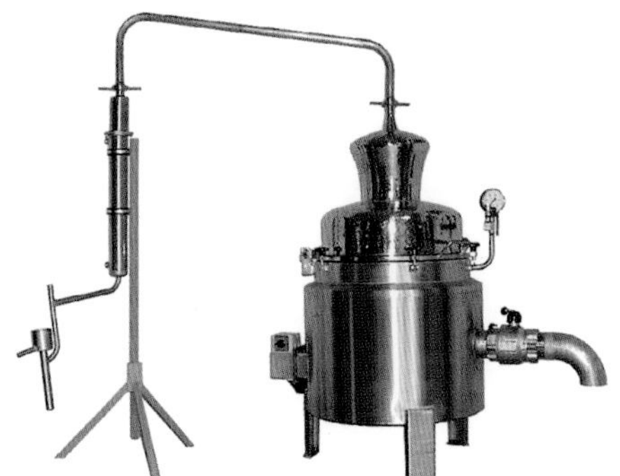

Stainless steel version—no patina.

Spirit Tube or Riser Pipe

This pipe is called a riser pipe because it is supposed to rise to the cooler. Here, too, some cooling takes place and water and fusel oil precipitate on the inside of the pipe and run back into the still-head and on into the boiler.

When purchasing a still, therefore, one should ensure that the still head is sufficiently large and that the riser pipe really does rise to the cooler.

Cooler (*Condenser*) and Sight Box

The purpose of the cooler or condenser is to liquefy the passing vapor. It must be engineered so that the vapors are completely cooled and condensed. The distillate (*raw or refined schnapps*) must flow out cold. If the distillate runs out warm there is partial loss of alcohol and aroma. The old cooling systems were often poorly designed.

The following types of coolers are used today:

Select cooler size so that distillate runs out cold.

Coil Cooler

In general these are coils of copper tubing in a cylindrical water tub. Cooling effectiveness is very good. Their chief drawback is that they are difficult to clean. After long standing periods, patina forms in the copper tubing and this finds its way into the distillate.

Plate Cooler

This consists of plate-like metal discs in a cylindrical metal housing, which sits in cool water. In addition to effective cooling, it has the advantage of easy cleaning. The plate rack can easily be removed for cleaning.

Tube Cooler

Warning: hard water can cause calcification!

This consists of a vertical tube bundle, washed round by cooling water. The vapor mixture condenses in the tubes. Very hard water can result in calcification of the tubes. One should therefore be able to open the cooler easily for decalcification.

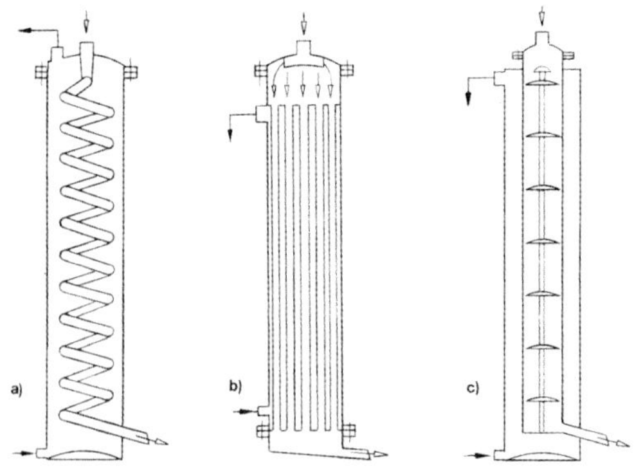

Types of coolers:
a. Coil cooler b. Tube cooler c. Plate cooler
→ cooling water → vapor entry or condensate exit

Some stills use two coolers: a cooler for the fore- and after-runs and a cooler for the middle-run. The second-run cooler is therefore always free of first and final run products.

Water Flow to the Cooler

This must always come from below. The cold water must be present where the distillate leaves the cooler, and the warm water is conducted up and away. The distillate leaves the cooler through a discharge pipe and runs into a prepared container. The disadvantage of this is that some liquid must always be captured in order to measure alcohol content. If larger quantities are being distilled, a so-called sight box is highly recommended. This is simply attached to the distillate discharge tube on the cooler.

Sight box.

Sight Box

The sight box has a recess which houses the alcoholometer. This makes it possible to read the alcohol strength at any time. The sight box is covered by a glass dome, preventing the loss of alcohol and aroma. The flow of distillate from the cooler to the receptacle should be as short as possible with minimal contact with the air (*loss of alcohol, aroma*). Never allow the distillate to splash freely into an open container.

The sight box should be removed before the head is collected so that no head remnants remain in the box, or use a sight box with a bottom drain.

TYPES OF STILLS

There are two types of still:

- **Simple Stills** consist of a boiler, head, riser pipe, and cooler. Two distillations are required (*raw and fine brandy*).
- **Simple Stills with Enhancement System** (*column device*). One distillation is sufficient.

Heating Methods

- Direct heating with single-wall boilers
- Indirect heating with oil and water bath boilers
- Electric heating with oil and water bath boilers

Distillation system with column

The greatest advantage of electric heating is precise heat control, and no heater connection is required. This type of boiler is somewhat more expensive than fired oil or water bath boilers. Before purchasing an electric boiler one should consider the available power connection (*approx. 15 kW*) and the local cost of electricity. If the business has its own source of fuel, a fired boiler will surely be more economical. Another thing to consider is the fact that an electric boiler transmits no heat to the distillation room. If the distillation room has no heating, which is often the case, a fired boiler is advisable. This is an important factor, especially if the room is also used to ferment the mash. The heat from the fired boiler will provide a warm room for subsequent mashes.

Heating must be well regulated in order to adjust it to suit the distillation process.

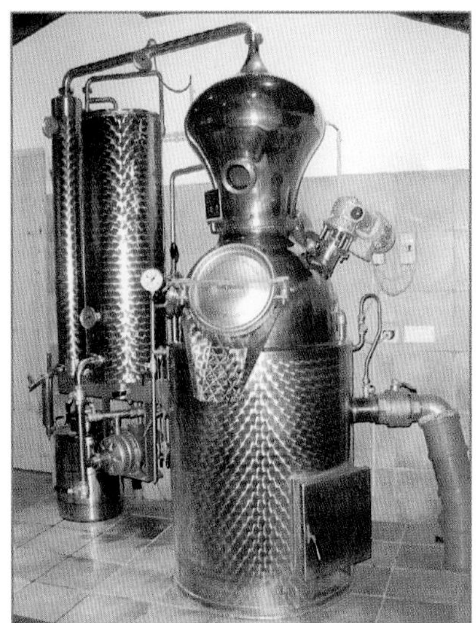

Distillation system with ball head

Distillation system with reflux condenser

Simple still

From experience, the power consumption of an electric boiler with a capacity of 103 liters (~27 gallons), distilling **raw brandy is approximately 30 kWh/boiler filling** and about **40 kWh/boiler filling for distilling fine brandy.**

Still with wood-fired boiler.

BOILER DESIGN

Single-Wall Boiler

For a long time this was the only type of boiler. The mash and the fire are separated by a single layer of metal, and thus the mash is heated directly. The fuel is used to its fullest capabilities, however, this type of boiler has a serious disadvantage in that viscous mashes can easily burn. The resulting substances are transferred to the brandy and reduce its quality, which can make it undrinkable. In this case even charcoal treatment is of no use. This type of boiler requires a coarser mash and heating must be carried out gently and cautiously.

Viscous mashes burn easily, and taste is transmitted to the distillate.

Double-Wall Boiler

Double-wall boilers are becoming increasingly popular because they offer solutions to the disadvantages of single-wall boilers. Depending on the filling material, they are also called water bath or oil bath boilers. The fire first heats the filling material, and this transmits the heat to the mash. Under certain conditions the mash in an oil bath boiler may still burn (*especially during emptying*), therefore a water bath boiler is a better choice for a commercial distillery. The mash cannot burn and emptying of the boiler can proceed very quickly.

To ensure that all of the alcohol is out of the mash, the temperature of the water in the water bath must be higher than 212°F (100°C). This is accomplished by achieving an overpressure of up to 0.5 bar (7.25 psi) in the completely sealed water bath. A safety valve must be installed to prevent the pressure from rising any further.

Water bath boilers offer good heat transfer without burning.

Gas and oil heating have proved very effective, as they permit automatic temperature regulation. Accurate temperature control makes it possible to achieve even distillation.

Filling and Emptying the Boiler

This job must be accomplished quickly and with no particular difficulties. This is especially important for commercial distilleries, so that the specified distilling time can be fully exploited. The boiler must have a sufficiently large opening for filling. In addition, a hopper can be attached. It should also be possible to quickly open and close the filler cap. In many cases the filler opening is formed by removing the head. There are also boilers with separate filler openings.

The ideal method of filling the boiler is to use a mash pump.

Basically there are three possible ways of emptying the boiler:

- Empty by tipping the entire boiler—this is done very quickly and easily.
- Discharge spouts on the bottom of the boiler leading to the side. The diameter should be at least 6 to 8 inches (*15 to 20cm*), so that even viscous stillage (*residue left by distillation*) can be emptied easily.
- Scooping out stillage from old brick boilers is rarely seen today. This method of emptying is very time consuming and is not advisable.

During distillation itself, care should be taken to ensure that all parts of the boiler are sealed tight. Even a minor loss of vapor can result in a significant loss of alcohol.

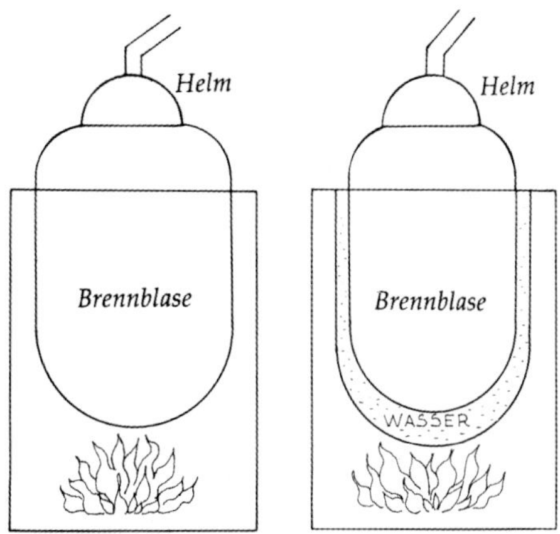

Boiler schematic: single-wall (left), double-wall (right).

To fully exploit the mash, temperature in the water bath must be higher than 212°F (100°C).

Filling the boiler using a hopper.

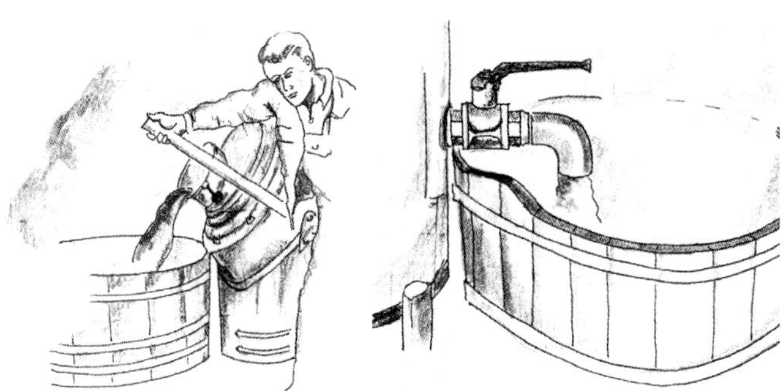

Emptying by tipping (left) and discharge nozzle (right).

SPECIAL EQUIPMENT

The simple still can be fitted with special equipment.

Special Equipment

1. Water bath to 0.5 bar (7.25 psi)
2. Drain cock or tipping device
3. Agitator (*stirrer*)
4. Tube, through which steam from the water bath is conveyed to the boiler (*steam transfer tube*)
5. Oil, gas, or electric heating
6. Oil bath
7. Fractionating systems, which consist of a maximum of 3 distillation stages and a reflux condenser (*fractionater*).

When an enhancement column is installed, just a single distillation run is required.

Column Devices (*Enhancement Systems*)

In order to obtain a higher percentage of alcohol from a simple still (boiler, head, riser tube, and cooler), it is necessary to distill a second time.

Special enhancement systems have been designed so that a high-percentage distillate can be obtained from a single process. The enhancement system or column contains bubble-top, sieve, or other plates. The allowable number of plates is specified in the applicable statutes of each country. The individual plates can be switched on or off, providing various control options when distilling with a single column.

They have the following advantages compared to simple stills:

- One distillation is sufficient to produce a high-percentage and pure distillate.
- This results in reduced working time.
- Heat and water consumption is reduced.

Disadvantages:

- Higher purchase costs.
- The distillation process is somewhat more complicated.

How does the enhancement (*fractionating column*) work?

The alcohol-water vapor mixture (*raw brandy*) rises from the still and enters the first tray, which is in a water bath. The alcohol-water vapor mixture must pass through the liquid, which causes it to cool, thereby losing mainly water (*which has a higher boiling point than alcohol*) and causing the alcohol concentration in the vapor to rise. This is roughly equivalent to refined brandy.

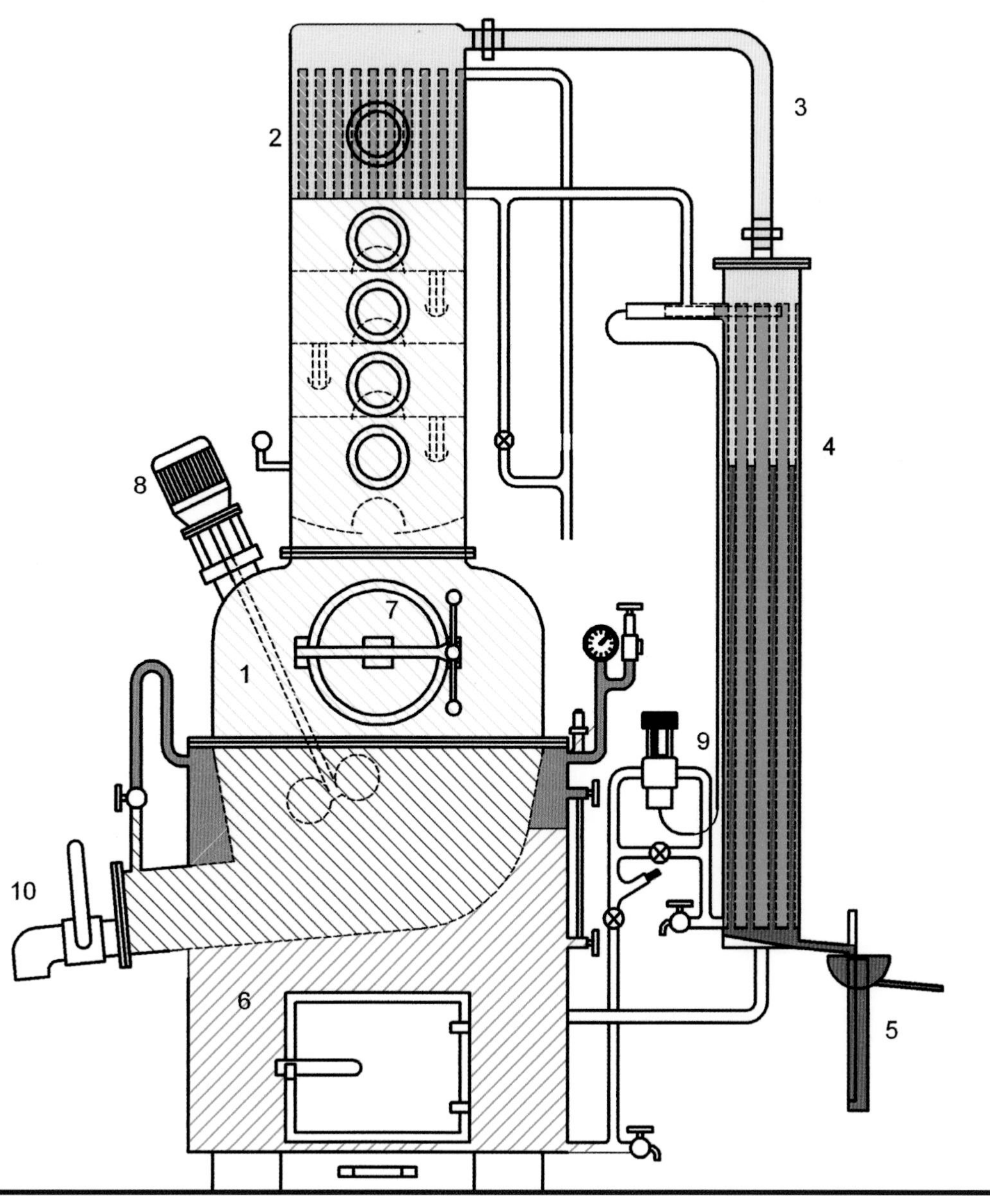

Water Bath Still with Enhancement Column, Holstein Company

1. Boiler
2. Head
3. Riser pipe
4. Cooler
5. Sight box
6. Water bath with fire box
7. Filler opening
8. Agitator
9. Cool water automatic system
10. Mash discharge nozzle

Each enhancement plate causes condensation and vaporization.

The alcohol-water vapor mixture passes through the second tray, again cools somewhat, water condenses and alcohol content again rises (*equivalent to a second refined brandy*).

It then passes through the third tray with the same process of alcohol enhancement (*third refined brandy*).

If a reflux condenser is present, further cooling results in additional condensation of water and another increase in alcohol concentration. If the column is used in this way, the result is a high-percentage distillate but one with minimal aroma substances.

By switching plates and reflux condenser cooling on and off, an aromatic distillate can be produced, depending on the raw material. Each plate and the reflux condenser remove substances with higher boiling points (*by-products*).

On some stills the level of the liquid in the plates can be regulated. "Simmer" means a low fluid level. The vapor passes quickly through the shallow fluid layer, resulting in reduced alcohol concentration but increased preservation of aroma.

Alcohol concentration rises from plate to plate.

On the "Boil" setting there is more liquid in the plate, thus more runback and a higher alcohol concentration.

Distilling with a column is a game with the bubble plates (*or other fractioning plates*) and the reflux condenser. The equipment manufacturer will provide recommendations for use.

Reflux Condenser

The reflux condenser is also called the pre-cooler, as it is located in front of the cooler. Reflux condensation is defined as partial condensation.

Reflux condensation = partial condensation, vapor becomes more alcohol rich.

The reflux condenser is also an additional enhancement system. Basically, reflux condensers are water coolers of various types (*cisterns, tube systems*). The cooling surface varies depending on the type and is regulated by the water level (full, one-half, or one-third full). The greater the cooling, the more vapor condenses and runs back into the boiler. More water (higher boiling point) than alcohol runs back, however.

The remaining vapor becomes richer in alcohol, thus the distillate is also richer in alcohol when it leaves the cooler.

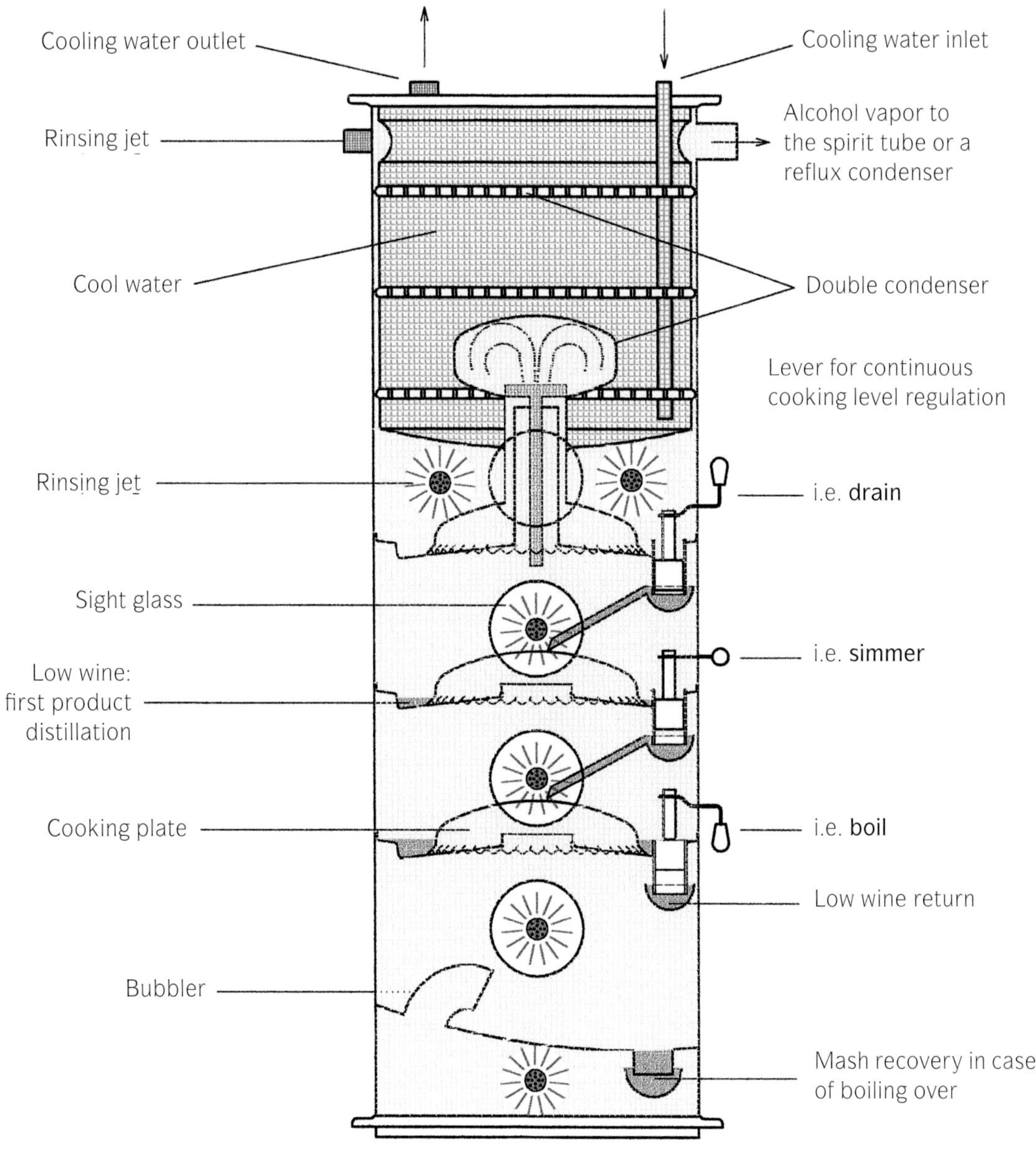

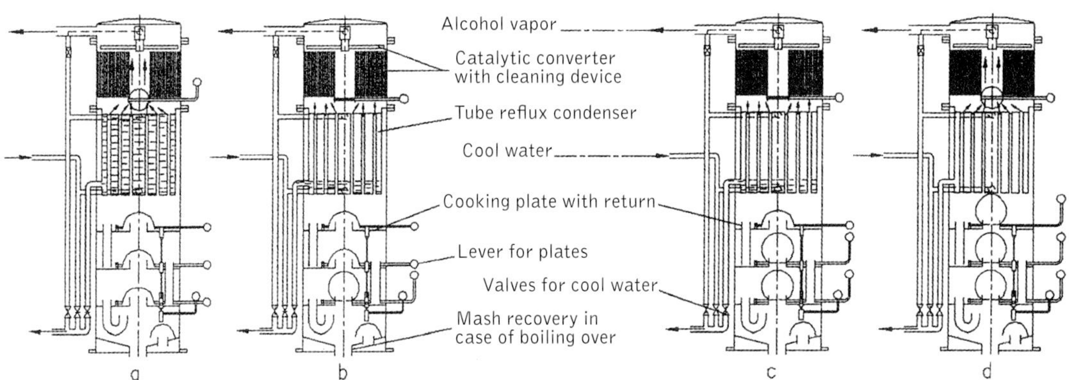

Enhancement System (*column*) with Controllable Bubble-top Plates, Reflux Condenser, and Catalytic Converter (*A. Holstein*).		
Column Settings	Effect	Usage
a) All plates and reflux condenser in full operation. Catalytic converter deactivated.	Highest alcohol concentration, greatest purification, slight aroma preservation	Brandy made from wine yeast, must, and grains
b) 1 plate disabled, reflux condenser partially disabled, catalytic converter enabled. (1/3 effective cooling surface)	Low percentages, rich aroma in distillate, reduced ethyl carbamate	Brandy made from stone fruits and pome fruits
c) 2 plates disabled, reflux condenser partially disabled, catalytic converter enabled. (1/3 effective cooling surface)	Low percentages, high levels of aromas preserved in distillate, reduced ethyl carbamate	Brandy made from stone fruits and pome fruits
d) All plates and reflux condenser disabled. Catalytic converter disabled.	Less purification and flavor amplification	Spirits and herbal brandies
e) Examples a) through d) can be combined in various combinations.		

If too much cooling takes place, the alcohol content rises, however, the aroma suffers.

The correct middle road must therefore be found.

There are no precise instructions for use, each still must be tested, sampled, and notes made about the best result. The result should have plenty of aroma and sufficient alcohol.

For those who add a reflux condenser to their still (without column), Constant A still applies for distillation duration. When used properly, even by itself the reflux condenser certainly has its advantages.

Catalytic Converter

Not permitted in Austria. Check your local laws before using.

In Austria catalytic converters are forbidden for simple stills. The catalytic converter consists of copper fins or copper packing with a large outer surface area. This provides intensive contact with the steam flowing through. The prussic acid in the steam is bound as copper cyanide complex and is prevented from entering the distillate. To retain its effectiveness, the copper must always be shiny—thus be well cleaned.

Operating Conditions of a Fractionating Column by U. Kothe

Operating Condition	Effect of the Enhancement	Use of the Enhancement
All bubble-top plates in the "Boil" position and heavy cooling by the double reflux condenser	Highest alcohol concentration, least aroma preservation, and maximum purification	Distillation of mealy materials, must, Jerusalem artichokes, and wine yeast
All bubble-top plates in the "Simmer" position and medium cooling by the double reflux condenser	Slightly weaker, aromatic distillate	Manufacture of fine brandies from stone and pome fruits
All bubble-top plates in the "Drain" position and cooling by the double reflux condenser only after 65% vol.	Little fortification but purification	Manufacture of spirits and herb brandies
All bubble-top plates in the "Simmer" position and medium cooling by the double reflux condenser; cartridge catalytic converter turned on	Small amount of low percentage, aromatic distillate; reduction of ethylcarbamate; increased purity	Mainly for distilling stone fruit, acetic pome fruit mashes and sulfured wine yeast, wine, and pomace
These examples are combinable in many variations.		

CLEANING OF STILLS

Cleanliness is an important prerequisite for the production of a quality distillate. This, of course, also applies to stills. While a still with a shiny exterior is pleasing to look at, when it comes to quality brandy, the interior is of more importance. The copper must shine, so that it can absorb sulfur compounds and cyanide.

Cleanliness = precondition for a good distillate.

Precipitates form on the copper which must be removed. Copper is consumed in this process, as copper compounds form in the boiler. Shiny copper also acts as a catalyst. It can bring about transformations in the mash or low wine without being consumed itself.

Prior to the distilling season, the boiler must only be steam stripped, as it should have been thoroughly cleaned after the last season. The steam should pour out of the sight box for at least fifteen minutes.

Basically one needs two different agents for cleaning:

- an **alkaline agent (lye)** for removing fatty deposits. Soda, caustic soda, P3, and products available in specialty stores are suitable.
- an **acidic agent** to remove various deposits and to neutralize after an alkaline cleaning. Citric acids are suitable.

Dirt in the still can result in distillate problems.

With some contaminants one must test to determine whether the alkaline or acidic cleaner will work.

Cleaning of Individual Components

After each distillation one should clean the still with water and a soft brush. Cleaning with an alkaline agent is recommended between distillations. The copper must always be bright and shiny so that sulfur compounds and cyanide can be absorbed.

An especially thorough cleaning should be carried out before distilling refined brandy. During this process, any lack of cleanliness will have a negative effect on the distillate. The cooler and riser tube, in particular, are prone to contamination. Wash everything out with a 0.5% caustic solution. Pull a bottle brush through the spirit tube and cooler and fill with a caustic solution. Also, wash the boiler and head with a caustic solution and then rinse well with warm water. Fill the coil cooler with caustic solution, let stand for some time and then wash well. A steam jet cleaner with reduced pressure (*about 1015 psi [70 bar]*) is also suitable.

Lye and acids are required for thorough cleaning.

Steam cleaning between distillations is always beneficial.

For cleaning copper surfaces, apply a 10% citric acid solution on warm parts and quickly rinse off. Treat stainless steel with caustic solution or a specialized steel cleaning agent. Modern stills have an apparatus for automatic cleaning. The manufacturer provides the necessary instructions for use (*e.g. the C. C. Carl Company*).

Consider the Following:

Before beginning the following cleaning process, ensure that:

- boiler, head, and column are equipped with spray heads,
- the tubing has a central connector,
- an acid- and alkaline-resistant pump with suitable connectors and hose is available.

Ideal feature: built-in cleaning jets for automatic cleaning.

To ensure proper circulation, the pump must be installed and connected so that suction can be applied at the stillage outlet and the pump's pressure fitting is connected to the central water spray connector. This installation causes the cleaning solution to collect at the deepest part of the boiler (*stillage outlet*), from where it can be injected back into the system.

First the boiler, head, and column should be clean and free of solid particles such as skins, pits, mash residue, etc.

Five Steps of Cleaning

Place the various cleaning solutions in the boiler and allow to circulate for 10 to 15 minutes.

- Step 1 Flush with water, if possible hot water with a temperature of about 158°F (70°C), for two minutes.
- Step 2 Flush with a caustic soda solution or dishwashing solution (temp. approx. 140°F [60°C]) for about 10 to 15 minutes (longer if necessary).
- Step 3 Flush with warm water for about 5 minutes.
- Step 4 Flush with 2 %mas citrus acid solution for about 10 minutes at approx. 86°F (30°C).
- Step 5 Flush with warm or cold water for about 2 minutes.

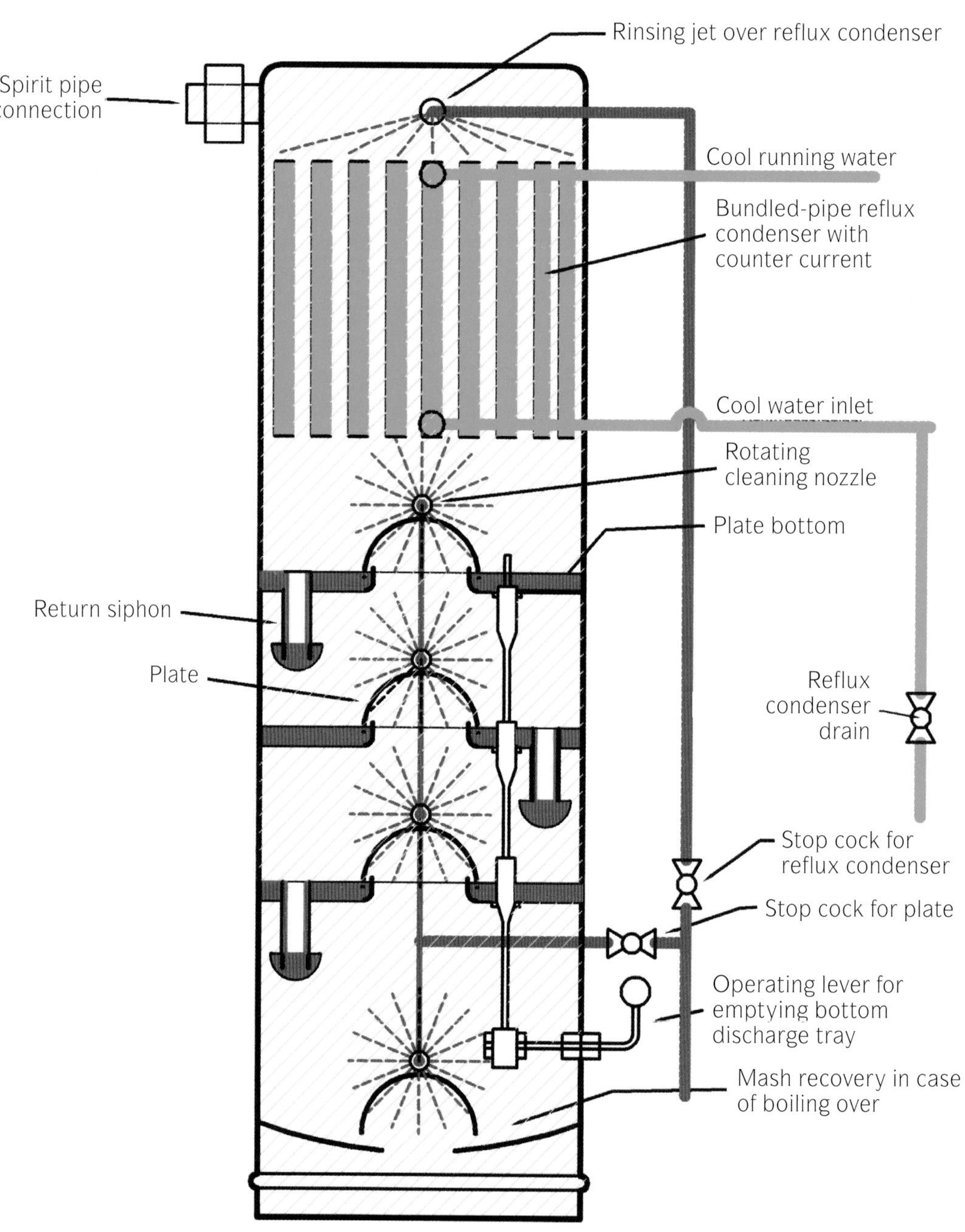
Rinsing jet over reflux condenser
Spirit pipe connection
Cool running water
Bundled-pipe reflux condenser with counter current
Cool water inlet
Rotating cleaning nozzle
Plate bottom
Return siphon
Plate
Reflux condenser drain
Stop cock for reflux condenser
Stop cock for plate
Operating lever for emptying bottom discharge tray
Mash recovery in case of boiling over

Distilling the Mash

...WITH SIMPLE STILLS

If all of the work until now has been carried out in an orderly fashion, the mash contains the desired materials that will produce the distillate. Through distillation, the potable alcohol (ethyl alcohol) and the good aroma and flavor substances will be separated from the other components of the mash and enriched. The quality of the distillate depends very greatly on the distillation process, however, all the distilling skill in the world is of no use if the mash is not in order. Good quality can only be obtained from a properly processed mash. Any minor or major errors committed on the way to a fermented mash have a deleterious effect during distillation. Even the best still cannot eradicate such errors. In itself, producing a quality brandy from a good mash presents no particular difficulties; one must only have a thorough knowledge of the distillation process and adhere to several important points.

What happens during distillation?

The fermented mash is heated. All liquid substances are turned into steam. The steam contains alcohol plus good and bad substances. The good and bad substances must be separated in repeated distillations. With a column still a single distillation cycle is sufficient to achieve separation.

Types of Steam Flow

Essentially there are two types:

- **Direct Flow Distillation:** in simple stills the steam flows from the boiler in the direction of the head, riser tube, and on to the cooler.
- **Counter Flow Distillation:** This takes place in simple stills with an enhancement system (*column*). The steam from the boiler rises, partially condenses in the column (*in the enhancement plates*), and runs back. Therefore steam is always rising, while some condensation is running back into the boiler.

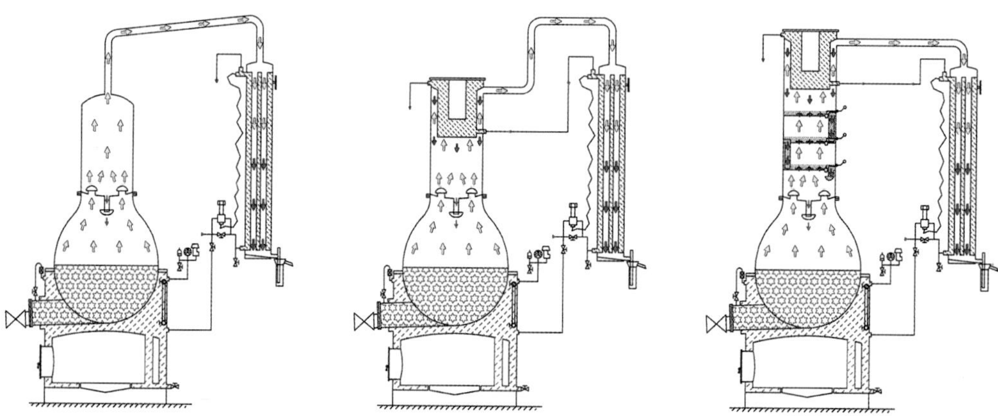

Direct flow distillation/combination/counter-flow distillation , ➜ vapors, ➜ condensate

Boiling Points of Various Elements Present in Low Wine	
Acetaldehyde	68.36°F (20.2°C)
Ether	95°F (35° C)
Acetone	133.88°F (56.6°C)
Methanol	148.28°F (64.6°C)
Acetate	171.5°F (77.5°C)
Ethyl Alcohol	172.94°F (78.3°C) (ethanol)
Water	212°F (100°C)
Fusel Oil	76-320°F (80-160°C) and higher alcohols
Acetic Acid	244.4°F (118°C)

COMPONENTS OF THE MASH DURING DISTILLATION

Liquid Components

The following substances are found in the raw brandy during the distillation process: water, ethyl alcohol (*potable alcohol*), methyl alcohol (*methanol – poisonous*), acetic acid, acetate, higher-order alcohols (*fusel oil*), acetaldehyde, prussic acid (*from stone fruits*), aromatic substances (*about 70 different ones*), ester, etc. These liquid substances are separated in subsequent distillations.

If using a still with enhancement system, separation takes place during a single distillation cycle.

Separation of volatile substances takes place during the second distillation.

Non-Liquid Components

Solid or dissolved substances from the fruit, such as parts of cells, salts, acids, etc. They remain in the boiler as residue.

FUNDAMENTALS OF DISTILLATION

Water and alcohol, the main components of the fermented mash, have different boiling points. Under normal conditions, water boils at 212°F (100°C) and alcohol at 172.94°F (78.3°C). When the mash is heated, water and alcohol evaporate simultaneously, but as alcohol has a lower boiling point, more alcohol vaporizes than water. This is true up to 172.94°F (*78.3°C*), the boiling point of alcohol. If there is further heating, the temperature approaches the boiling point of water, causing the water component of the steam to rise. Further heating is therefore senseless, especially during the second distillation.

Because of their different boiling points, it is possible to separate good and bad substances.

The remaining liquid substances vaporize along with the water and alcohol. Here, too, the boiling point and the mixture ratio with other substances play a role. The substances with lower boiling points, such as acetate and acetaldehyde, vaporize as soon as heating begins; those substances with a higher boiling point than potable alcohol do not vaporize until later at higher temperatures (*higher-order alcohols = fusel oil*). By distilling twice, it is possible to separate the various liquid substances in such a way as to obtain a good distillate, by removing the undesirable substances. Proper temperature control is vital to the removal of unwanted substances, especially during the second distillation.

Submit all necessary forms to the relevant government agencies in a timely manner.

FIRST (*RAW*) AND SECOND (*FINE*) DISTILLATIONS

Depending on local laws, commercial alcohol production must be reported to the responsible government agency prior to the start of distillation.

When using a simple still, a second distillation is absolutely necessary to produce a good quality, flavorful brandy. In distillation with a column still, a single run is usually sufficient, however, when distilling an alcohol-poor mash (*elderberry, Rowan berry, etc.*), a first and second distillation are more advantageous.

The mash is in the final stage of fermentation or is completely fermented. If fermentation was interrupted, a fermentation test was carried out (see pg. 66). If preparation and fermentation were conducted properly, there should be no layer of mold on the mash. This can develop if a mash is stored too long without acid treatment and is exposed to air. This skin should be removed. Poor mash (*acescence, mold, bad smell, etc.*) should never be mixed with healthy mash.

The addition of water is only necessary with viscous mashes.

Addition of Water

In some cases it is necessary to thin the mash with water. When using a single-wall boiler

Old-fashioned stills.

without agitator, the mash must be very thin to prevent burning. If there is an agitator, but especially if using an oil or water bath boiler, much thicker mashes can be used. Excessively thick mashes are bad, as evaporation is more difficult to achieve.

With enzyme-treated mashes, the addition of water is generally unnecessary, as they are already very thin.

With foaming mashes (*such as elderberry or other incompletely fermented mashes*), it is advisable to add an anti-foaming agent as per the directions.

First (*Raw*) Distillation

Separation of volatile and solid substances.

The purpose of the first distillation is to separate the liquid from the non-liquid substances. Heating of the mash causes the liquid substances to evaporate. They pass through the riser tube into the cooler and there are cooled and liquefied. The pure distilling time per boiler differs greatly. It depends on the size of the boiler and also on its design. A ballpark figure for pure distilling time is 2 to 2 1/2 hours.

Distilling too quickly is damaging to the aroma. Too much water is vaporized, and it takes too many undesired elements, such as higher alcohols and fatty acids, with it.

The use of an agitator makes for rapid warming of the mash. The agitator is left on until distillation is well under way.

Alcoholometer in the sight box.

A temperature of 158°F (*70°C*) can be reached quickly. At this point the heat should be reduced so that the subsequent rise in temperature is slow. This is particularly important so that the alcohol and aroma substances have time to escape.

The product of the first distillation is called raw brandy. Its volume is equal to 1/4 to 1/3 of the mash volume. When distillation begins, alcohol content is about 40 to 60 %vol, depending on the fruit used. In the entire first distillate the alcohol content is between 20 and 30 %vol, and sometimes even less.

Filling the boiler (with low wine) by hand.

Alcohol content varies greatly as it depends on the raw materials, mash quality, and the addition of water.

End of the First Distillation

The first distillation has ended when the alcohol content of the escaping distillate is no more than 3% vol. Extracting all of the alcohol from the mash would take too much time and fuel, and the liquid component of the mash would become too watery. As well, toward the end of the distillation process, increasing amounts of unwanted substances could be transferred to the distillate. In years when fruit yields are good, one might perhaps stop somewhat sooner than in poorer years. There are dedicated raw brandy meters which provide accurate readings even at these low alcohol contents (*measuring range: 0-10% ABV*).

The raw brandy contains all the volatile substances from the mash.

Contents of the Raw Brandy

These are mainly potable alcohol and water, plus, depending on mash quality, good and sometimes bad aroma substances, fusel oil, acetate, etc. The raw brandy is cloudy and tastes disharmonious and unpleasant. Three to four first distillations yield sufficient raw brandy for one boiler for second distillation. First, however, one distills more of the same mash and collects the liquid so that several second distillations can be carried out.

Clean the boiler well prior to second distillation, especially the riser tube and the cooler, so that no unwanted substances make their way into the refined brandy.

Second distillation: separation of the desired and undesired substances.

Second (*Fine*) Distillation

The second distillation is to increase alcohol content, clean the raw brandy, and separate the good aroma substances from the bad. This is achieved through fractionated distillation.

Distillation Process

Heating must be introduced very slowly to enable a good separation of the various ingredients. As a rule of thumb, the distillate should begin dripping from the cooler after about an hour. Only through gradual heating can the unwanted substances with low boiling points (*acetaldehyde, acetate, some methyl alcohol*) be evaporated first. The distillate should also not pass too quickly through the middle-run. If conducted properly, the second distillation takes at least four hours.

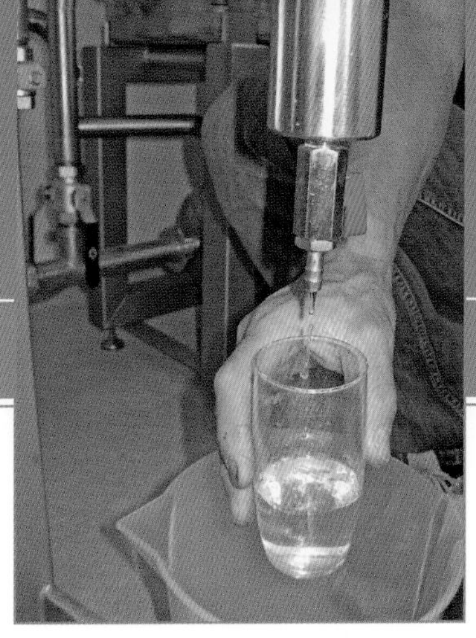

Capturing the head (from the outlet on the bottom of the sight box).

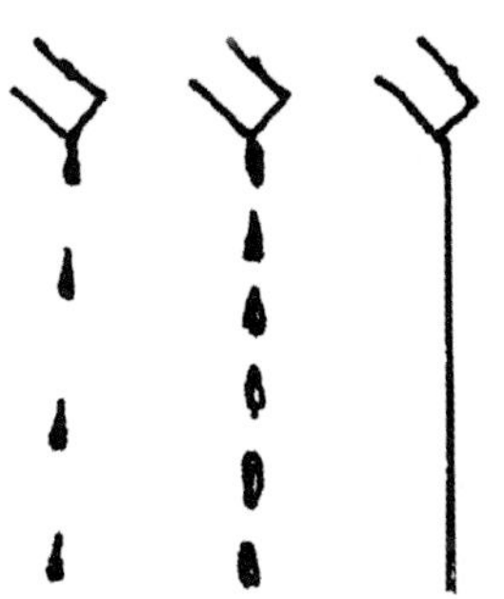

This is how the fore-run should begin.

Rushing the second distillation is the biggest mistake in making fruit brandy, making it impossible to obtain good qualities even with a good mash. The refined brandy is collected in three parts (*fractions*).

1 THE FORE-RUN (HEAD)

When heated slowly, it contains mainly volatile substances like aldehyde, acetate, and some methyl alcohol. The head also contains some potable alcohol and aromatics, the more so the faster the heating-up process. With apples in particular, but other fruits as well, the aromatics are transferred at the beginning of distillation and some find their way into the head, instead of the heart where they actually belong.

During the second distillation heat slowly so that the distillate begins dripping from the cooler after an hour.

If there is no bottom drain, remove the sight box to collect the head so that a clean separation is achieved. Residue from the head and tail often remain trapped in the cooler and can contaminate the heart. This can be prevented by using two coolers and a three-way cock. One cooler is for the head and tail, the other for the heart.

It is impossible to determine exactly when the head ends and the heart begins. The notion that the head ends when the distillate becomes clear is not entirely true. Only by tasting can one determine when the head is finished. It is also impossible to predict the head volume with certainty. This depends, in particular, on the quality of the mash, the speed of distillation, and the alcohol content of the mash. Given a good mash, the alcohol content is approximately 1% more or less of the low end.

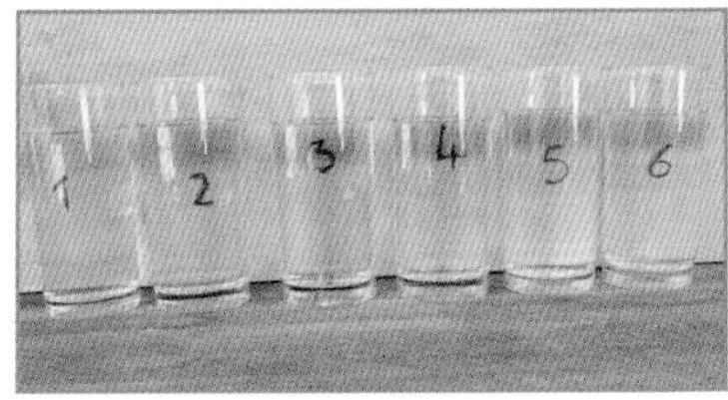

Head in numbered glasses.

Determining the Quantity of Head from a 100-Liter (26.4-gallon) Boiler

One begins with a half percent = 1/2 liter (*~2 cups*) of head. Then six to eight 1/4-liter (*~1 cup*) glasses are filled and numbered. With a 50-liter (*13.2-gallon*) boiler one begins with a 1/4 liter and then six to eight 1/8-liter (*~1/2-cup*) glasses.

Testing the fore-run (smell & taste), beginning with the second glass.

If the mash was poor, it is necessary to draw off somewhat more. The more head one has to take away, the more aromatics and alcohol are missing from the heart. Under no circumstances, however, should one add the head to the heart on account of the aromatics.

Tasting the Head

The head contains volatile substances. The smell is pungent, reminiscent of glue, and the taste is very sharp. Beginners should begin practice tasting with an experienced distiller.

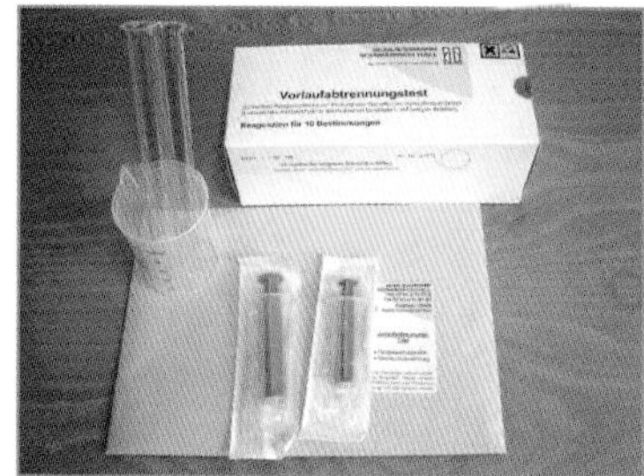

Fore-run separation test.

Begin with the last test glass. Place some head in a schnapps glass and thin with warm water to about 40% ABV (*1 part head and 1-1.5 parts water*). Now test each glass one by one until the head smell and the typical taste appear. From that glass to Glass 1 everything is head. If, for example, there is a hint of head taste in the fourth 1/4-liter test glass, this test sample can be added to the next batch of low wine. Now one knows approximately the amount of head in the same mash. In this area one uses 1/8-liter glasses. In our example, therefore, after the third quarter-liter glass, one-eighth-liter glasses are used.

Head Testing Device

For those unwilling to rely on their sense of taste, the end of the head can be determined using Prof. Pieper's head separation test. The basic equipment with reagents is available from specialty stores.

Use of the Head

The head should be collected separately and never added to the next refined or second distillation. This will only result in an increase in unwanted substances, and separation becomes increasingly difficult.

The head can be used to mix an herb liniment, for dressing wounds, etc.

THE MIDDLE-RUN (HEART)

As soon as the distillate tastes pure, the middle-run or heart has begun. It should be collected in a separate container with minimal exposure to the air, It begins running at about 70% ABV. The heart contains the substances that produce a drinkable distillate.

Also called the heart.

Here it is particularly important to distill slowly. As distillation proceeds, the alcohol content slowly drops. It is impossible to determine with certainty when the heart ends and the tail begins. Tasting is the surest method. One simply dips a finger and tastes. With experience, one can recognize the tail products and then switch to the final run.

When Does the Middle-Run End?

Depending on mash quality, distillation speed, and type of fruit, the first tail products such as fusel oil (*higher alcohols*) can begin appearing from 55% ABV, and consequently taste testing can begin. For those who are uncertain about "*finger testing,*" beginning at 55% ABV the distillate should be captured in quarter-liter glasses until 45% ABV is reached. Taste testing will then reveal the separation between the heart and tail.

Finger taste test during the switch from middle-run to after-run.

Some good aroma substances may also find their way into the after-run.

With some fruits (such as Rowan berries), the tail will contain a batch of good aromatic substances. In this case, after switching the distillate one should capture it by the quarter liter and taste test. In this way, later aromatic substances can still be used. If several batches of distillate are made from the same low wine, after the initial second distillation, the distiller will have a better idea of when to switch.

When small licensed distillers allow the second run to continue until the entire heart has reached a strength of about 50% ABV, the effect on quality is extremely negative. By that point the heart contains too much tail with fusel oils and other undesirable substances, resulting in diminished quality. The heart is equivalent to approximately 30% of the boiler contents.

3 AFTER-RUN (TAIL)

The tail runs until the distillate indicates 4 to 5% ABV. By then the contents of the boiler contain almost no alcohol (*0.1–0.2% ABV*). The tail contains higher levels of fusel oil with unpleasant taste and aroma substances. Every brandy maker should occasionally taste the tail, to see for himself the drop in quality. If mash quality is poor, one should stop at 8 to 10% ABV.

After switching to after-run, the distillation process can be sped up.

Use of the Tail

The tail is roughly similar in quantity (*25-30%*) to the heart. Its alcohol content is about 20%.

Only in exceptional cases should you add the tail to the next second distillation.

There is a variety of uses for the tail:

a) If little tail accrues, it can be added to the low wine of the following second distillation. This should only happen two or three times, after which the entire tail should be discarded.

b) The better method is to separately distill the tail once again. Fore-run separation is determined by taste-testing. The middle-run should be ended 5% ABV sooner than during a normal second distillation (*see Point C*) and the tail discarded.

c) With aromatic fruits (*such as Williams Christ pears*), the head often contains high levels of aromatic substances. In this case the head and tail are collected and distilled together. Once again heat slowly, so that a good head separation is possible. When distilling the head and tail, one should end the middle-run 5% ABV sooner than during a normal second distillation. If one switched to after-run at 50% ABV during second distillation, one should now switch at 55% ABV. Taste-testing should be carried out at the proper time and the tail discarded.

Subsequently, distill tail again by itself and then utilize accordingly.

If, during the procedures in Points b) and c), the quality of the heart meets the requirements, it can be added to the middle-run of the next second distillation. The heart that has been captured as after-run can be made into juniper berry brandy (*see "Juniper Berries," pg. 126*).

One should never, however, mix bad quality material with good. The good quality will lose more than the bad quality will gain.

Further Uses of the Second Middle-Run

If the quality requirements are met, it can be sold as second quality.

It can undergo charcoal treatment (see pg. 103) and be used for the production of liqueur. If this is the intention, the charcoal treatment should be carried out prior to distilling the tail.

Adding the tail to the next second distillation is no solution.

Maturing the Heart

The heart tastes rough and unbalanced, and its aroma is also unsatisfactory. Storage serves to develop and mature the distillate.

Before setting the drinkable strength, the heart should be stored in the dark for at least six to eight weeks at a temperature of 59-68° (*15-20°C*). Some oxygen is also necessary for maturation. It is sufficient if the aging containers are not completely filled and are loosely sealed. Maturation of the distillate can also be achieved at lower

Distillate storage—glass balloons.

temperatures, however this takes more time. If one has sufficient stocks, however, a longer aging period (*1 to 2 years*) is an advantage.

For the distillate to become a good brandy, it must first be aged.

During maturation, some acetaldehyde (*fore-run product*) combines with ethyl alcohol to form acetal, a substance with an unpleasant smell. Some higher-order alcohols can also be transformed into aromatic substances. This does not mean, however, that one should reduce the separation of the fore- and after-runs, for only small amounts of good aroma substances are transformed. After a time the heart loses its somewhat raw and unbalanced taste. It becomes milder, rounder, and more palatable. If the distillate is stored at too high a temperature and in open containers, the result is loss of alcohol. Rapid temperature changes are undesirable. The storage room should also be dark.

Brandies are sometimes stored in oak casks. Neutral distillates are best suited to this type of storage. Distillates with a fine aroma should not be used for cask storage. If they are, they should be removed before acquiring a woody tone.

During cask storage the distillate absorbs wood substances, and new, pleasant-smelling compounds are created. There is also discoloration of the distillate. The length of storage must be checked by taste testing.

Exception:

The heart derived from Williams Christ pears should only be stored for a short time (*3-4 weeks*), with little exposure to the air and below 59°F (*15°C*) (*see pg. 127*).

Storage in wooden barrels.

It is difficult to predict the effects of aging. The process varies based on the distillate and storage conditions. Personal experience is therefore important. These maturation processes, which lead to a significant improvement of the distillate, take place very slowly and continue in the diluted distillations in the bottle. Top brandies (*excluding Williams Brandy*) should be allowed 2-3 years to age. To date, all attempts with artificial aging processes have failed.

Old "modern" still with an enhancement system (*column*).

DISTILLING THE MASH IN A COLUMN STILL

A single distillation is sufficient because of the plates installed in the column. Switching the plates on and off and use of the reflux condenser make it possible for the distiller to adjust the process. The manufacturers have developed various enhancement plates. Good advice is definitely required before purchasing a column still.

In almost all cases, while the alcohol content rises as more plates are in operation, the aroma substances unfortunately drop. The setting of the reflux condenser is also important. An additional strengthening can be achieved by cooling the distillate correctly. This is necessary if plates are switched off.

The possible operating conditions may be seen in these two charts/diagrams:

- Still made by the Kothe Company, which controls strengthening the distillate with the settings "Simmer" or "Boil" (pg. 85), and
- Still made by the Holstein Company, which controls the process by turning bubble-top plates on and off (pg. 84).

These settings are guidelines and can be varied at any time. Through one's own experiences and experiments with various settings, every owner of a column still must become a master.

The purchase of a still with enhancement system (column) must be carefully considered.

Before purchasing a column, one must realize that distilling with a column still is more difficult. Buying a column still in the hope of distilling quickly is a mistake. The quality of the resulting product will not be what was desired.

Distilling without a column is undoubtedly simpler. With a simple still, an error during the first distillation can be corrected during the second. With a column still that is not so.

The fundamentals of distillation also apply to a column still. The good contents of the mash must be separated from the bad.

The mash must be heated slowly, so that the fore-run products can escape. After an hour, the head can begin running slowly. The reflux condenser is set to provide little or no cooling, so that the volatile fore-run products are not retained.

The aroma substances of Williams Christ pears are extremely volatile and migrate to the head. This can be held back somewhat by light cooling at the reflux condenser. Capture the head as describe on page 95 and taste test.

Glass balloon for storage of distillate.

The volume of head depends on the raw materials, the mash quality, and the distillation process. If everything is correct, 1/2 liter of head can suffice (*with a 150-liter [39.6-gallon] still*). The more errors that are made, the greater the volume of the head (*up to 1/2 l, 1 l, or more*). Once again, only taste testing can reveal when it is time to switch to after-run. Like the fore-run, it is dependent on the same factors and is at 70-75% ABV. The tail is distilled down to 5-10% ABV.

The amount of head depends on mash quality and speed of distillation.

The use and handling of the head, heart, and tail are the same as in distillation without a column. A thermometer reading before the cooler is recommended. One can observe the temperature at which the after-run begins (*determined by taste testing*) and can then use this as a benchmark.

Testing is important, as no precise directions are possible. Accurate notes should, however, be kept about the various settings and distillation results. Exchanging experiences with other column distillers is also important.

STORAGE CONTAINERS

The containers used to store fruit brandies must be alcohol resistant and be flavor neutral.

Storage in wooden casks is not common. A wooden cask (*oak, damson wood*) can be used for special products. The distillate absorbs substances from the wood and acquires a special tone.

Stainless steel distillate storage vessel.

- Glass balloons in various sizes—20, 30, and 50 liters etc. are available. Glass is completely neutral to alcohol and has no effect on flavor. Because of their various sizes, they are particularly well suited to smaller quantities. Their only disadvantage is the threat of breakage.
- Glazed earthenware containers are also very well suited.
- Stainless steel tanks are also flavor-neutral and alcohol resistant.
- Certain plastic containers, whose makers certify them suitable for the storage of distillates. Maximum acceptable alcohol concentrations must be certified for the containers.

Acescence (*Sourness*)

Flavor Defects

Acrolein Taint

Distillation Errors

Most errors have the following causes:

- poor raw materials selection (unripe, rotten, moldy, dirty);
- improper mash preparation, mashing temperature too cold, poor yeast preparation, additives (yeast, enzyme, acid, yeast salt) were not added or were used improperly or in insufficient quantity;
- unsuitable fermentation vessels and poorly executed fermentation;
- errors during distillation—poor separation of the head, heart, and tail, rushed distillation. These errors can be corrected by distilling again;
- unsuitable fermentation vessels and poorly executed fermentation. Poor sealing, wrong material, poorly cleaned, incorrect fermentation temperature, mixing mashes too frequently.

Recommendation:

Next distilling season observe everything closely from raw materials selection to mashing to distillation. Then nothing will go wrong.

Most errors can be eliminated beforehand by following proper working procedures. If a poor mash turns up, it should be distilled separately and not mixed with good mash.

Never mix poor distillates with good, for the latter will lose quality. They should be utilized separately, and they should never be sold.

ACESCENCE (*SOURNESS*)

Vinegar bacteria need oxygen, therefore seal fermentation vessels properly and install airlocks.

Acetic acid can form through exposure to air or long storage. This reduces alcohol and gives the distillate a sour taste.

Binding the Vinegar

Acetic acid can be bound with pure calcium carbonate (*available in drugstores*). Add 0.44 lb (200 g) to 26.4 gallons (100 liters) of distillate or low wine; the low wine is then distilled as normal. When added to distillate one waits a few days until the excess calcium carbonate has settled. One then draws off the clarified distillate, leaving the white residue on the bottom of the container, filtering it. No more than 200 grams of calcium carbonate per 100 liters should be used, otherwise the flavor can suffer. If there is strong acescence, for which 200 grams of calcium carbonate per 100 liters is insufficient, the acid content should be measured first. In this case deacidification must take place in the low wine.

FLAVOR DEFECTS

Flavor defects are caused by dirty fruit, unclean fermentation vessels, and poorly-cleaned stills.

If the distillate has a flavor defect, it can be treated with charcoal. It is better to carry out this treatment at the low wine stage; it is, however, possible with finished distillate. One uses 50-100g/l of deflavoring or activated charcoal.

Use of Charcoal

Mix the charcoal well with a small amount of liquid (distillate or low wine), add the remaining liquid and stir everything. The charcoal settles after a short time; therefore one can soon taste-test to determine whether sufficient charcoal has been added or if it has helped at all. If not, add additional charcoal. This should not be seen as absolutely necessary, however, as aromatic substances are also bound in the process. Stir frequently, and after two days at the latest siphon off the low wine or distillate from the charcoal sediment. The distillate is filtered if necessary, and the low wine is distilled. The charcoal must not be distilled with the low wine, otherwise the bad flavor substances will reenter the alcohol vapor. Charcoal treatment is most effective in distillates that are less then 50% ABV.

ACROLEIN TAINT

Immediately noticeable during distillation—pungent smell and burning of the eyes.

This defect has become more common in recent years. Various types of bacteria can create acrolein, which has an extremely strong odor, from the glycerin in the mash. Acrolein has almost the same effect as tear gas. Its boiling point is 111.2°F (44°C) and during distillation it vaporizes immediately. The resulting distillate is unpalatable (sharp burning taste). During distillation the nasal and mucous membranes can become so irritated that the process has to be halted.

From soil bacteria on fruit that has come into contact with the ground.

Causes

The cause of bacteria infection can be traced back to unclean raw material which has been contaminated by dirt. Additional microorganisms enter the mash, forming more substances which negatively affect quality. Acrolein taint is usually not detectable prior to distillation; it is only released and noticed once heating begins.

The contamination can be spread from container to container as a result of stirring. Never mix acrolein tainted mashes with healthy ones, as this will spoil the healthy mash.

Eliminating the Defect

This problem can be solved by storing for several months in an open container with good exposure to the air. Frequent stirring also helps. Serious acrolein contamination cannot be fixed and the distillate remains undrinkable.

...expose to air for minor defects, serious defects are uncorrectable.

The best way to avoid most defects is to work cleanly and carefully, beginning with the selection of raw materials, to distillation itself. Every defect has a serious impact on quality, which cannot be restored even by appropriate treatment.

For the small commercial distiller it is usually very difficult to recognize and treat many defects. Should something happen, however, one should bring in a good practitioner, an agricultural or winemaking advisor.

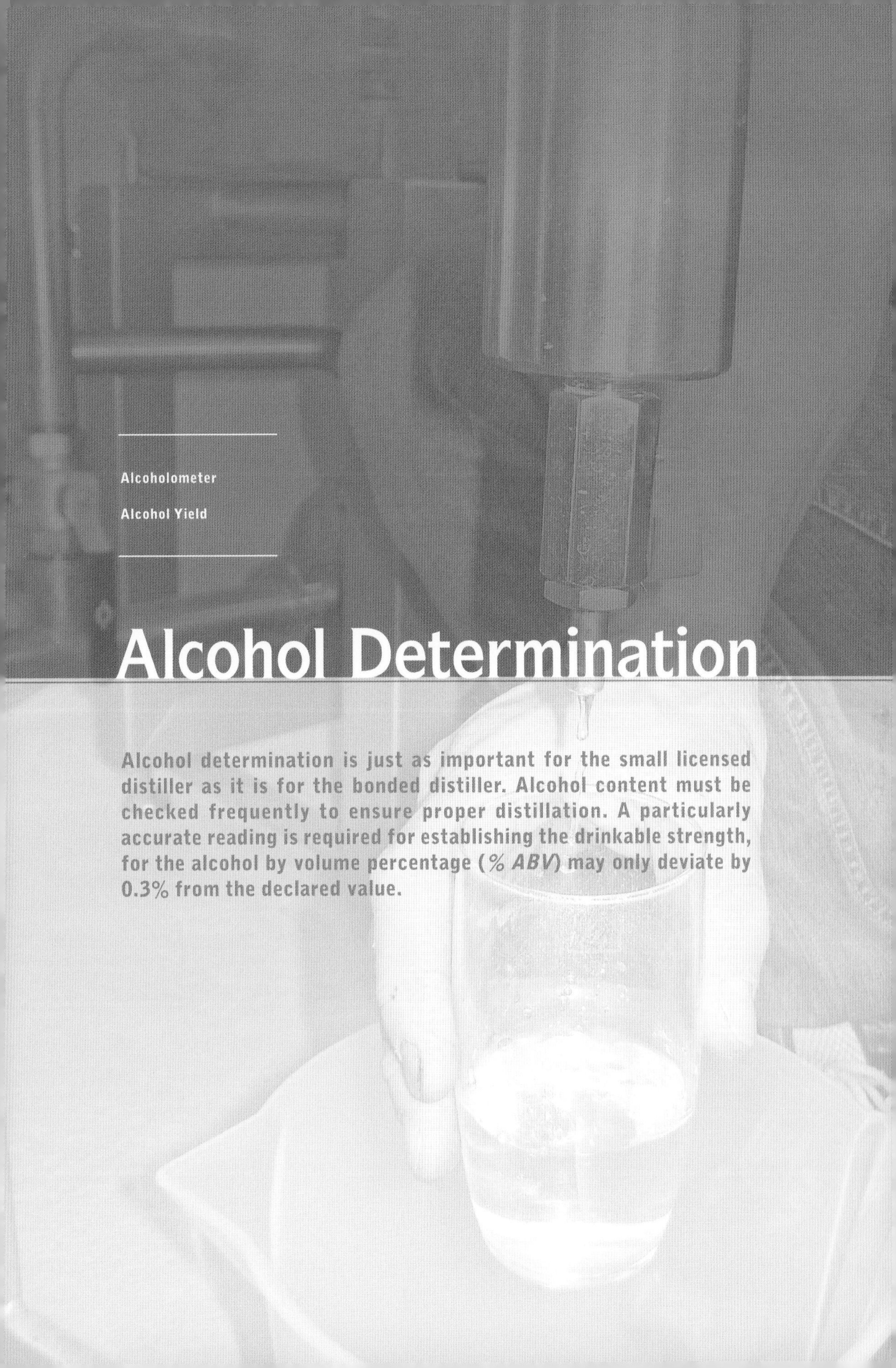

Alcoholometer

Alcohol Yield

Alcohol Determination

Alcohol determination is just as important for the small licensed distiller as it is for the bonded distiller. Alcohol content must be checked frequently to ensure proper distillation. A particularly accurate reading is required for establishing the drinkable strength, for the alcohol by volume percentage (*% ABV*) may only deviate by 0.3% from the declared value.

Alcohol content can be expressed in two ways:

a) in Mass Content = %mas (*formerly Percent by Weight*). It expresses how many kilograms of alcohol are present in 100 kilograms of distillate. If a value of 50 %mas is given for a distillate, it means that 100 kg of distillate contains 50 kg of alcohol. Distilleries do not usually use mass content, however.

b) in Alcohol by Volume = % ABV. How many liters of alcohol are there in 100 liters of distillate? If a value of 50% ABV is given for a distillate, it means that there are 50 liters of pure alcohol in 100 liters of distillate.

As one liter of alcohol/water mixture (AWM) weighs less than a kilogram, there are significant differences.

Example

A distillate with 51.9% ABV has 44.3 %mas alcohol. Purely optically, expressing the value as alcohol by volume is more favorable, therefore the alcohol content of all alcoholic beverages is expressed as alcohol by volume.

ALCOHOLOMETER

The alcohol content of extract-free distillates, such as accrue in the distillation of fruit mashes, can easily be measured as a volume percentage by using an alcoholometer. The standard measuring temperature is 68°F (20°C). If the temperature of the distillate is lower than 68°F (20°C) the reading will be too low, while a temperature higher than 68°F (20°C) will result in a reading that is too high. The best method is to place the distillate in a warm room with a temperature of 68°F (20°C), which permits accurate readings to be taken. If the distillate's temperature is not 68°F (20°C), only the apparent alcohol content can be read.

Using an alcoholometer to measure alcohol content.

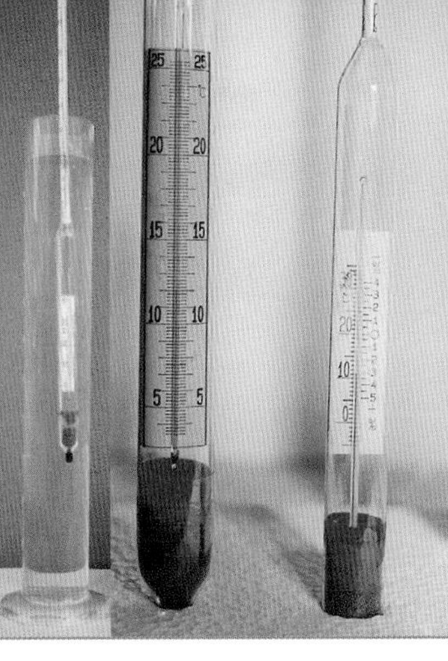

Alcohol measurement: the alcoholometer must be floating freely when the reading is taken.

Example

Reading (*apparent alcohol content*):
42% ABV
Measuring temperature:
53.6°F (12°C)
Alcohol content at 68°F (20°C):
45.1% ABV.

The true alcohol content can be read from the Correction Table for Determining Alcohol Content (*volume concentration*) at 68°F (20°C) (see pg. 136).

There are also alcoholometers whose built-in thermometer is equipped with a temperature correction scale. A correction value is given for each temperature and this must be added or subtracted to the base reading. The resulting values are too imprecise for a precise measurement, as required for sale.

With a temperature variation of 4.5°F (2.5°C) the deviation is approximately +/- 1% ABV.

Purchasing an Alcoholometer

In the European Union there is binding legislation which states that only officially calibrated percentage-by-volume alcoholometers may be used for the public sale of spirits. The measuring temperature is specified as 68°F (20°C).

The "EU Percentage by Volume Alcoholometer" must have a measuring range no greater than 10% ABV, for example 40-50% ABV or 50-60% ABV. The divisions are 0.1% ABV. The graduations on the scale are spaced so that readings in increments of 0.1% ABV can easily be taken. Each spindle has an

The following nine pieces of information are present on the spindle of an "EU Alcoholometer":

1. Percentage by Volume Alcoholometer
2. DIN 12803
3. %vol. (% ABV)
4. Ethanol
5. 20° C
6. Class I, II, or III (three different levels of accuracy)
7. Manufacturer's name or emblem
8. Serial number
9. E (*the Greek letter epsilon is the symbol for EU type approval and shows that the instrument is approved for use in the EU*)

Left: correction scale
Right: temperature scale

integral thermometer, which is important for temperature correction.

Calibrated alcoholometers have an "e" etched on their surface to indicate that they have been calibrated. The year of calibration and the national emblem of the country in which the calibration took place must also be visible.

Anyone who sells fruit brandy needs an accurate alcoholometer, in some places the maximum allowable deviation from the advertised alcohol content is only +/- 0.3%.

These EU alcoholometers are not strictly required by small licensed distillers, but they do need an alcoholometer that can be or has been calibrated for a measuring range of 40- 50% ABV (*possibly also 30-40% ABV*) and has a reading accuracy of 0.1% ABV and a built-in thermometer. The alcohol content of ready-for-sale brandy must be accurate to within +/- 0.3% ABV, and for this an accurate alcoholometer is necessary.

If the stated alcohol content is 43% ABV, the actual content must be between 42.7 and 43.3% ABV.

Older alcoholometers with a calibration temperature of 15.56° C (60°F) should no longer be used.

For alcohol-weak liquids (*tails, low wine*) there are low wine gauges with a measuring range of 0-10% ABV.

Sufficiently large measuring cylinder and an alcoholometer that has been or is capable of being calibrated.

Measuring Procedure with an Alcoholometer

One needs a sufficiently large measuring cylinder whose height is determined by the length of the alcoholometer. For an EU alcoholometer with a maximum measuring range of 10% ABV (e.g. 40-50% ABV), the cylinder height is 350 mm (13.77 inches) and has an approximate diameter of 33-34 mm (1.29-1.33 inches) for approximately 200 ml (6.76 oz) of fluid. The alcoholometer must be able to move freely. It is very important that the alcoholometer and measuring cylinder are completely clean (*especially free of grease*) and dry.

The clean alcoholometer must be able to move freely.

The distillate is slowly poured into the cylinder, which is tilted to prevent the formation of small air bubbles that could affect the reading. Hold the alcoholometer over the cylinder and let it slide slowly into the distillate until the spindle is floating freely. The end of the spindle must be at least 2 cm (3/4 inch) from the bottom of the measuring cylinder. If the alcoholometer is inserted too quickly, it can strike the bottom of the cylinder and be damaged.

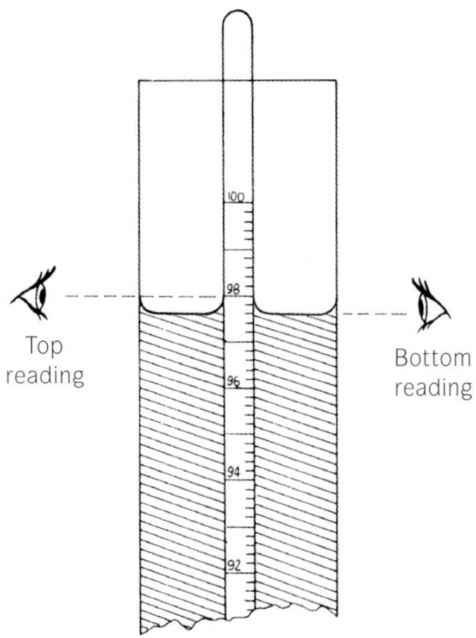

It must be stressed again that only extract-free distillates can be measured in this way. Pure distillates are alcohol-water mixtures, for which alcoholometers are made. The small quantities of other substances, such as higher-order alcohols, volatile acids, aromatic substances, etc., that are in the distillate have no effect on the accuracy of the readings. If the distillate contains sugar or other extract substances (in liqueurs), however, alcohol measurement with an alcoholometer is not possible. If not stated on the alcoholometer, "reading bottom" applies.

If the reading is to be taken at the top, this will be indicated on the alcoholometer. The designation top or bottom indicates whether the raised edge of the liquid is to be included in the reading or not.

ALCOHOL YIELD

For every brandy maker, it is important to know how much alcohol is obtained from 100 liters of mash. This can be calculated very easily.

Calculating alcohol yield is a good self-check to ensure that proper procedure has been followed.

One requires the following values:

a) the alcohol content of the distillate at 68°F (20°C) = A

b) the quantity of distillate = B

c) the quantity of mash, in liters, that was distilled (*according to the report submitted to the customs office or relevant government agency or by weighing*) = M

$$\text{The alcohol yield per 100 l of mash} = \frac{A \times B}{M}$$

Example

76 l (20 gallons) of distillate with 48% ABV at 20°C (68°F) from 1400 kg (3086 lbs) of mash

$$\text{Yield} = \frac{A \times B}{M} = \frac{76 \times 48}{1400} = 2.60 \text{ liters of pure alcohol/100 l mash}$$

$$\text{Yield} = \frac{A1 \times B1 + A2 \times B2 + A3 \times B3}{M}$$

For a precise yield calculation, the fruit should be weighed before mashing. The fruit price is calculated in kilograms and the mash later in liters. For pome fruits, 100 kg yields approximately 100 liters of mash, while for other fruits one requires 105-110 kg of fruit for 100 liters of mash.

For a precise yield, the raw materials must be weighed—estimating is not good enough.

Water Quality

Calculating the Amount of Water

Adding Water

Adjusting the Drinking Strength

Generally the heart has an alcohol content of 60-70% ABV. This alcohol content must now be reduced to drinkable strength. It is up to the individual to decide how strong his/her brandy should be, however, an alcohol content of 41-43% is recommended. At this strength the burning taste is no longer as strong, while the aroma is still robust.

Cloudiness

One must be aware of the danger of cloudiness or hazing as alcohol content drops. The probability of hazing is high, especially below 45% ABV. Cloudiness should be avoided if at all possible, because it is usually associated with a reduction in quality as flavoring substances are lost.

Use soft water, hard water over 5° dH (5.21 grains of calcium carbonate / gallon) leads to hazing. Water from primitive rock is ideal.

If the maker lacks the resources to clarify (*filter*) his product, he/she should conduct tests with a small quantity of brandy to determine at which alcohol level the distillate begins to cloud. The test sample should be left in a cool place for two or three days to allow the contaminants to settle and avoid secondary hazing.

The strength of special brandies, such as gentian, Rowan berry, masterwort, and others, should be set no higher than 45% ABV. In general it can be said that in future a rather lower alcohol content will be desired.

Austrian law states that the minimum permissible alcohol content of a fine or noble brandy is 38% ABV. Check your local regulations for relevant standards.

WATER QUALITY

The water used must be free of hardening substances (*calcium and magnesium*). These substances are insoluble in an alcohol solution and cause hazing. Water from primitive rock is usually free of hardening substances and can be used.

If someone knows from experience that his/her tap water does not cause hazing or affect the flavor of the distillate, he/she can confidently use this water.

In any case, the water used must be flavor-neutral. Generally water up to 5° dH (*German degree of hardness*) can be used (*equal to 89.24 ppm of calcium carbonate or 5.21 grains of calcium carbonate / gallon*).

The following options are available for hard water:

- Use the boiler to distill the required quantity of water, filling it with water instead of mash.

Water softener (binds calcium and magnesium).

The distilled water is completely free of salts but tastes rather bland and soon begins to smell musty.

- Treat the water with a water softener, which binds the unwanted calcium and magnesium salts. The sodium salts, which do not produce hazing, remain in the water. The resulting product tastes better than distilled water. Suitable small units are already on the market.
- It is also possible to buy softened water (*grocery stores and drugstores*).

CALCULATING THE AMOUNT OF WATER

Calculating the necessary quantity of water is not exactly simple, as mixing alcohol and water results in a volume reduction (*contraction*).

There are two methods of calculation:

Approximate Quantitative Determination through Calculation

After adding the calculated quantity of water, the alcohol content is measured, after which it can be corrected by adding small amounts of water. Precise measurement of the amount of distillate and the alcohol content are important (*take into account temperature*).

Example

First one works out the alcohol by volume at 20°C (68°F). 70 liters (18.49 gallons) of heart with 65% ABV, for example, results in 4550 alcohol percents (70 × 65). One then selects the desired strength, for example 42% ABV. One can then calculate the total quantity to be derived from the 4550 alcohol percents.

$$\text{Total quantity} = \frac{4550}{42} = 108.33\ \text{l of brandy with 42\% ABV.}$$

In this case, therefore, 108.33 l minus 70 l = 38.33 l.
The addition of 38.33 liters of water is required.

In reality, because of the volume reduction, one must use rather more water. As previously described, however, this can be adjusted later.

Account for a decrease in volume.

Determining Quantity Using Mixture Tables

A mixture table is used to determine the exact amount of water to be added.

Adding water to the heart leads to a volume contraction (volume reduction), which must be taken into consideration.

The volume contraction (volume reduction) is already factored in.

The table provides a sample calculation for 100 liters of distillate.

The table indicates the amount of water required to thin 100 liters of distillate to the desired alcohol content.

Taking volume reduction into account, one needs 1.25 liters more water than calculated in the above example (38.33 *liters of water*).

Example

70 liters heart with 65% ABV is to be adjusted to 42%. According to the table (pg. 138), 56.55 l of water are required for 100 l of 65% heart.

The formula for quantities smaller than 100 liters is:

$$\text{Quantity of distillate} \times \frac{\text{Quantity of water for 100 l}}{100} = \text{necessary quantity of water}$$

Necessary quantity of water for 70 l of distillate at 65% ABV. Alcohol:

$$\frac{70 \times 56.55}{100} = \frac{3958.5}{100} = 39.58 \text{ l water}$$

For the 70 liters of heart at 65% ABV, one requires 39.58 liters of water to obtain a brandy with 42% alcohol by volume.

ADDING WATER

If water is added incorrectly, the result can be cloudiness or hazing.

Adjusting the drinkable strength—slowly pour water into the distillate while stirring.

Always remember the following:

a) Water and distillate must be at the same temperature when mixed. This can best be achieved by allowing both to sit in the same room for several days.

b) The water is always poured into the distillate and never the reverse. The water should be poured into the distillate in a fine stream while stirring constantly.

If one thins in stages (*e.g. by 10% every 2-3 days*), larger particles will form which can be more easily removed by filtration.

Water and distillate mix slowly. If water is added too quickly, an alcohol under-concentration can occur where the water contacts the distillate, which can result in haziness.

An experienced brandy maker proceeds as follows when adding water: he/she pours the water into the distillate—as described above—until an alcohol concentration of about 55% is reached. The remainder of the water he/she adds by drops using a drip system (pipet or cock) on the container. Using this slow and gentle method, there is almost no hazing to 43% ABV. This makes filtration unnecessary and, what is particularly important, no aroma substances are lost with the hazing substances.

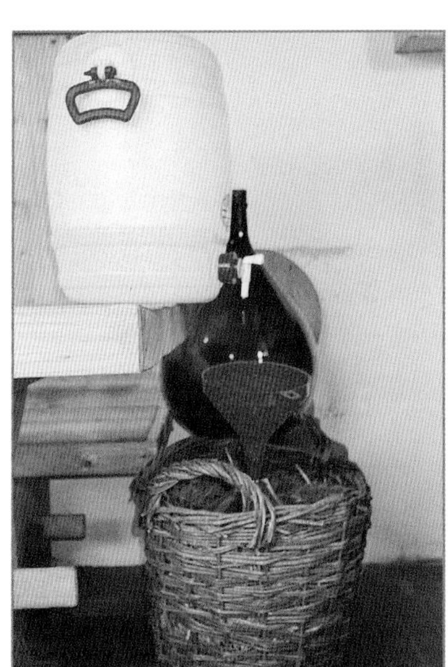

After proper mixing, the alcohol content is checked and, if necessary, corrected. It is advisable that not all of the water be added at once. This is particularly important if the alcohol content and quantity were not measured precisely. In this way, after checking, the alcohol content can be adjusted more precisely.

Adding water in drops to adjust drinkable strength.

Filtration Equipment

Clarifying or Filtering

Fruit brandy, or schnapps, is actually a "living" product. Various chemical reactions are constantly taking place, some of which are beneficial, while others can have a detrimental effect.

Funnel filter.

Every schnapps distiller knows that hazing can occur after the drinkable strength is set. The customer, of course, wants a clear brandy. It is not particularly difficult to eliminate this hazing by filtering, but in most cases aroma and flavor substances are lost with the clouding substances, which means that the brandy loses some quality. Through proper filtering, it is possible to produce a brandy that is capable of withstanding everything—cold, heat, light—without clouding again. But does it still have the same quality as before filtration? What is necessary is to find the right balance?

On one hand, everything should be done to produce a flawless brandy. This begins with the selection of fruit and affects everything from the mashing, fermentation, and distillation to the setting of drinking strength. If no mistakes are made and extreme care is exercised during distillation, a clear brandy can be produced without filtration. All that is left is to exercise care when setting the drinking strength (page 111).

Proper Storage of Fruit and Root Brandies

Customers are certainly in need of enlightenment when it comes to the storage of fruit and root brandies. A true fruit or root brandy does not belong in the refrigerator. A small label on the bottle with the notation "Do not store in the refrigerator, may cause clouding," or "This is a quality product and should be stored and consumed at room temperature" would perhaps make sense.

Thinning to less than 45% ABV often results in hazing. Substances (*fusel oil, ester, terpene, calcium and magnesium from poor blended water*) that are only soluble at higher alcohol concentrations precipitate. These cannot be removed by simple filtration.

Storage in a refrigerator can lead to hazy discoloration.

How much should the distillate be cooled prior to filtering?

It must always be remembered that good aroma substances are removed with the hazing substances. Brandy distillers who sell direct to their customers can explain about the proper storage temperature (room temperature). In this case, cooling by 14.4-18°F (8-10°C) prior to filtration would suffice. Store the distillate at this temperature for 10-14 days and then filter at this temperature. For those unable to control storage temperature, the distillate should be cooled to between 32°F (0°C) and 23°F (-5°C). Store for one to two weeks and then filter at this temperature.

It is recommended that the distillate be thinned in stages (*e.g. by 10% ABV every three days*). In this way, larger hazing particles and droplets are formed, which are easier to filter.

Filter with candle filter (*Zeta-Plus*): Center, filter with candle filter for distillates; right, filter candle for juices; left, filter candle for water softening (*ion exchanger, reusable*).

Selective filtration with special filter sheets for undesirable particulate substances; loss of aroma substances is avoided.

Filters for Selective Filtration

Advances have also been made in the development of filter sheets and candles. There are filter sheets which make selective filtration possible. Certain haze-forming substances (*e.g. long-chain fatty acid esters*) are filtered out before hazing forms. Aromatic substances are spared in the process.

Using these special filter sheets, filtration can be carried out at plus temperatures between 41°F (5°C) and 59°F (15°C). The distillate is set at 42% ABV, for example. If no hazing appears, a test sample is placed in the freezer. If it becomes clouded, then the clear brandy is filtered with an appropriate filter sheet. The cause of the cloudiness is then filtered out. The cold test is then repeated.

There are various filtering options according to the quantity to be filtered. The matter of price must also be considered.

FILTRATION EQUIPMENT

Funnel Filter

The simplest method of filtration is a funnel with suitable folded filter. It is well suited for smaller quantities and is capable of "automatic filtration." The balloon bottle is positioned so that the end of the obliquely-cut drain hose is roughly at the same height as the rim of the funnel inside the folded filter. When filtration begins, the balloon bottle must be completely full and sealed absolutely air tight with a rubber stopper. In this way, the amount of fluid running from the continuously open hose is the same as that filtered. As soon as the surface level of the liquid reaches the mouth of the hose the feed stops. Also good for filtration below 32°F (0°C).

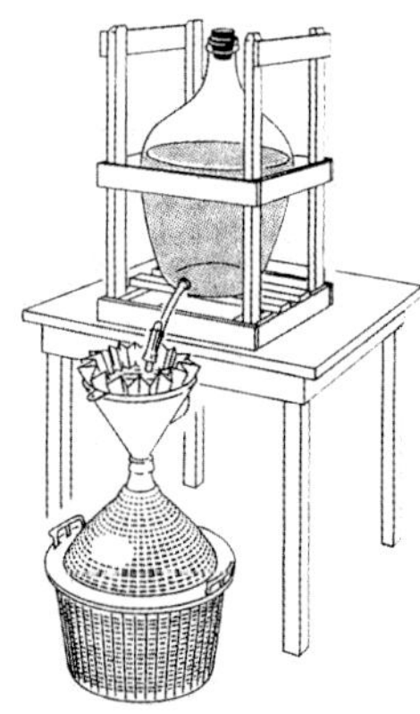

Funnel filter.

Filters with Filter Candles

Candle filters consist of molded plastic with various additions. They can only be used one time.

Enolmatik vacuum filler combined with filter candle.

Type Zeta-Plus

This is a small handy device, which is affordable and well suited for larger quantities. The filter is made of rustproof steel and plastic, with filtration through an asbestos-free fiber material. 100 to 200 liters of distillate can be filtered in an hour. The device works without a pump, and all that is required is a height difference of 1 to 3 meters (3.28 to 9.84 feet) between inlet and outlet. After use, the filter is washed out and after drying is stored until the next filtration. The filter candle can be obtained with pore sizes of 5.0, 1.0, and 0.45 micrometers. The candle is good for 2000 to 2500 liters (528 to 660 gallons), after which it must be replaced.

Tandem Candle Filter

The tandem candle filter can be combined with the Enolmatik vacuum filler. The candles come in various pore sizes, for various particulate substances.

Calitus Candle Filters (*with pump or just as a filter element*)

These can be attached to other filtration devices (*e.g. pumps*).

Sheet Filters

Sheet filters are round or square panels. They are made of various materials, like cellulose, synthetic resins, and perlite. Various pore sizes make it possible to filter the largest to the finest particulate substances.

Now available are extremely inexpensive 220-mm-diameter round filters for sheet filtration systems. These can be operated without a pump, using only a pressure differential (*height difference of 1-1.5 meters*). These filters are suitable for small and also larger quantities (*several hundred liters*).

Filtration by means of height difference and round filter sheet.

Vinamat filter—very suitable for small quantities.

The outlet from the filter should always be somewhat higher than the filter, so that there is always a certain backlog to the filter. This ensures that both filter plates are fully suffused. One can achieve a higher flow rate by raising the discharge hose or by placing the filter upright or at an angle.

After loading the filter, allow water to run through for 5-10 minutes until the water runs out tasteless.

It is important that the filter plates are installed correctly, so that the flow is from the large-pore to the fine-pore side.

Vinamat Filter

This is a small filter with two filter sheets and a five-liter tank with pump. It is very well suited for small quantities of distillate. It also functions on pressure differential.

Bottle Filling

Storage of Ready-to-Drink Distillates

Bottle Filling and Storage

For bottling, fruit brandy should be at a temperature of 68°F (20°C). Schnapps expands in the heat and contracts in the cold. 68°F (20°C) is the alcohol-measuring temperature and also the measuring temperature for determining filling quantity.

Bottle filling with an Enolmat vacuum filler.

BOTTLE FILLING

The simplest method is to elevate the container holding the brandy and fill the bottles using a hose and hose clamp.

One can also use a Simplex filling device. It is suitable for bottling, decanting, and filter feeding.

The Enolmatik Vacuum Filler is a simple and inexpensive device. It ensures that every bottle is filled to the same level. Its performance is entirely satisfactory for small distilleries.

STORAGE OF READY-TO-DRINK DISTILLATES

After the drinking strength has been set, the brandy should be stored in a warm, dark place for at least several weeks. Alcohol and water need to properly "sink their teeth" into each other. A well-aged brandy should taste smooth and harmonic. Sharpness and burning in the mouth and throat are not indications of quality. The finished brandy can be aged in bottles or larger containers.

Bear in mind when filling bottles that the alcohol can expand a great deal when heated and this can lead to bottle breakage. If one has sufficient stocks, cool storage is just as suitable, although aging takes somewhat longer.

For Rowan berry brandy, storage for several weeks at 68-77°F (20-25°C) is very advantageous. At that temperature it soon achieves its full aroma.

Glass balloon for distillate storage.

Drinking Culture

Various alcoholic drinks have an optimal serving temperature, at which their aroma, taste, and unique qualities can be appreciated.

Today almost every type of drink must be served cold. But let us reconsider and drink the various beverages at the proper temperature. Grain schnapps is drunk cold, but the qualities of the various fruit brandies only become apparent at higher temperatures (59-64.4°F [15-18°C]). They do not, therefore, belong in the refrigerator—unless they are of particularly poor quality.

In the past, brandies often had alcohol contents of 50% or greater. They were drunk from schnapps glasses and emptied in one drink. It was important that the brandy burned all the way to the stomach. In addition, it was not smelled or tasted.

Eye – clarity and color
Nose – aroma, variety, purity, flaws
Palate – purity, variety, taste, flaws

Today things are different. Brandy drinkers want to enjoy a quality brandy with the nose and palate. One needs a special glass, the so-called Fine Brandy Drinking Glass. The aroma substances develop in the bulged part of the glass and flow through a chimney-like opening to the nose. The glass is filled to the one-third mark. All of the senses should contribute to the enjoyment of a fine fruit brandy.

Proper tasting can be learned—where better than at a display of fruit brandies?

Good brandies should not be kept in large bottles. In opened bottles the aroma spreads to fill the empty space. Before pouring, therefore, tip the bottle several times so that the aroma returns to the brandy.

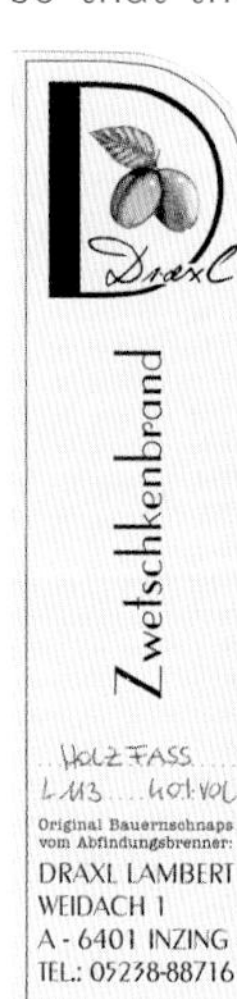

Special Brandies

In the previous chapters the preparation of various raw materials was described. In this chapter I will describe the processing of several raw materials into special brandies which today are highly prized by consumers.

Processing tips will only be offered when they differ from normal procedures.

Juniper berry, gentian, and masterwort are not regulated by Austrian law as they are mainly of local significance. But it is your responsibility to follow your own local laws regarding using these ingredients to make fruit brandy.

Juniper berry in fruit brandy
Masterwort in fruit brandy
Gentian in fruit brandy

As these raw materials are usually fermented in a fruit mash, these brandies can be designated as follows:

If fermentation takes place in an apple mash, the distillate can be named as such (*e.g. juniper berry in apple brandy etc.*). A **cleaning distillation** can also be made in which these substances are soaked in a tail or heart for several days and then distilled.

The aroma yield is better, however, if these raw materials are fermented with the rest of the mash.

4.4-11 lbs (2-5 kg) of juniper berries for 26.4 gallons (100 l) of mash, according to taste.

JUNIPER BERRY IN FRUIT BRANDY

First, one prepares a concentrated juniper berry low wine by fermenting the mashed berries (*put through a meat grinder or crushed*) with as much fruit mash as required to fill the boiler. The amount of juniper berries added depends on the desired strength of the juniper flavor in the finished distillate. Some like it strong, others rather milder. As a guideline, one can add 4.4 to 11 lbs (2 to 5 kg) of berries for every 26.4 gallons (100 l) of mash; one must also consider the quantity of finished distillate. In any case it is better to add more berries, as dilution with neutral distillate is always possible.

Sufficient normal low wine or tail is added to the juniper low wine to enable a fine schnapps to be produced. Before adding, the necessary tail can be treated with deflavoring charcoal.

Once again, sufficient head and tail must be removed during the second distillation. The heart with neutral distillate must be adjusted to the desired aroma strength!

It is perhaps advisable to make two different aromatic brandies. Alcohol content should be 42-45% ABV. If the essential oils cause problems during filtration, then reduce alcohol content by 5% ABV and store at 32°F (0°C) for one to two weeks. Afterwards, filter (*cold*) and finally adjust to the desired drinking strength with high-percentage heart.

MASTERWORT IN FRUIT BRANDY

The well-cleaned roots are ground in a meat grinder and fermented in an apple mash. If one requires larger quantities of masterwort brandy, one adds 6.6-11 lbs (3-5 kg) of fresh or 2.2-4.4 lbs (1-2 kg) of dried roots to 26.4 gallons (100 l) of mash (or enough to fill the boiler). After the first distillation, additional low wine can be added to fill the boiler for the second distillation. The resulting fine brandy can be cut with neutral distillate until the desired flavor intensity is achieved. It is beneficial to produce two different flavor intensities. The distillate is adjusted to 43-45% ABV. One can calculate approximately 0.73 lb (1/3 kg) of dried roots for 2.64 gallons (10 liters) of finished distillate.

GENTIAN ROOT IN FRUIT BRANDY

Preparation is essentially the same as for masterwort. For one boiler-full of mash (*26.4 gallons [100 l]*) one requires 4.4-6.6 lbs (2-3 kg) of fresh, washed, and well-mashed roots (*3/4 kg dried*). Approximately one kilogram of fresh or 1.65 lb (*1/3 kg*) of dried roots is required to produce 2.64 gallons (*10 liters*) of finished distillate. Again, for beginners, use more roots at first! The yellow gentian is already being cultivated commercially. Cultivation is possible to elevations of 5249 feet (*1600 meters*).

WILLIAMS CHRIST PEARS (*Williams Brandy*)

If properly prepared, this variety of pear produces an outstanding distillate. The pears must not be picked too soon. They should be close to eating ripeness and come from fruit producing areas where this variety develops its full aroma.

Mashing should take place when the pears begin to get soft. They must be easily squashed with the hand but must not be discolored (*brown*) inside.

For particularly fine brandy, the stems must be removed, as they can produce a slightly bitter taste in the distillate. In addition, the fruits should not use bruised, rotten, or green. Sugar content is not particularly high, coming in at between 7 and 10%, and the acid content is relatively low (*acidification required*). The aroma, however, is very marked. It is hardly noticeable in the mash but emerges strongly during distillation.

The low acid content (*pH value*) can result in problems during fermentation, therefore acid treatment (see pg. 51) is recommended. Adding acid lowers the pH level and inhibits many harmful organisms, while pure selected yeast works perfectly at low pH levels.

Enzyme treatment should be carried out to liquefy the mash and achieve better alcohol yield.

Use the appropriate acid preparations to set the pH value at about 3.0-3.2. Enzyme treatment should also be carried out to liquefy the mash. Add pure selected yeast (see pg. 43). When mashed, the pears should have a temperature of 60.8-64.4°F (16-18°C), so that the mash is at the correct temperature for fermentation.

Fermentation

Fermentation temperature is 59-64.4°F (15-18°C). Higher temperatures result in loss of aroma. If, after three to four weeks (*or sooner*), no more CO_2 is leaving the airlock, it is time to determine the degree of fermentation. This is accomplished by extract determination (*between 1.7 and 4 %mas*). Quicker results can be achieved with sugar test strips (*used for diabetes testing and available at the drugstore*) or by using Clinitest equipment.

The production of top fruit brandies requires a great deal of skill and experience.

Distillation

To achieve the optimal aroma yield, distillation must take place as fermentation is ending or immediately after it ends. Storing the mash for longer than this inevitably leads to loss of aroma and quality. Carry out the second distillation slowly and carefully! At 55% ABV in the fore-run, begin taste testing to determine if the distillate still tastes fine. From that point on, one can collect the distillate by the half-liter or liter and then taste. As soon as a fusel-oil taste appears in the distillate, switch to the after-run.

With Williams Christ pears one sometimes obtains good aroma substances below 40% ABV, however these are usually strongly mixed with fusel oils and thus cannot be used.

Storage

Store the heart in the dark for 1-2 months at about 59°F (15°C) with little exposure to air. Higher temperatures cause loss of aroma, and light leads to rancidness (*because of the essential oils*).

Adjusting Drinking Strength and Filtration

Essential oils often cause hazing problems in Williams Brandy.

Williams Brandy contains many essential oils, so that clarity is often impossible to achieve. If, however, one sets the distillate 4-5% ABV under drinking strength and after filtration adds a high-percentage heart to achieve the desired drinking strength, the slight haze disappears and one has a clear Williams Brandy.

Cooling Williams Brandy to 32°F (0°C) or lower before filtration is not advised, as this will result in the loss of too many essential oils and with them aroma substances. As a fruit brandy, and especially a Williams Brandy, does not belong in the refrigerator, there is no need for aggressive cooling before filtration; a temperature of 41-46.4°F (5-8°C) is sufficient. One company, for example, recommends a selective filtration with "Beco Select" filter sheets at 39.2-42.8°F (4-6°C). This process filters out elements (*e.g. fatty acids*) that can cause hazing (see pg. 116).

Storing the Ready-to-Drink Brandy

The correct degree of ripeness is important to quality.

The Williams aroma is sensitive to light, heat, and oxygen, therefore it must be stored in full containers in the dark at about 59°F (15°C)! Do not store in excessively large bottles, for slow consumption in half-full bottles leads to loss of aroma.

ELDERBERRY BRANDY

In addition to the wild-growing black elderberry there are already several good selections such as the "Haschberg" variety. The fruit is picked when there are no, or very few, green berries on the umbels. The berries must be separated from the stems mechanically or stripped over rabbit wire. If harvested too late, small stems are left hanging from the berries. These can enter the mash and result in distillation problems. One must subsequently process the berries with a mash mill to quickly reduce them to a pulp. If the berries are all mashed together, more frequent stirring is needed. Elderberry mashes have little acid and yeast nutrients and are therefore very susceptible to various fermentation problems.

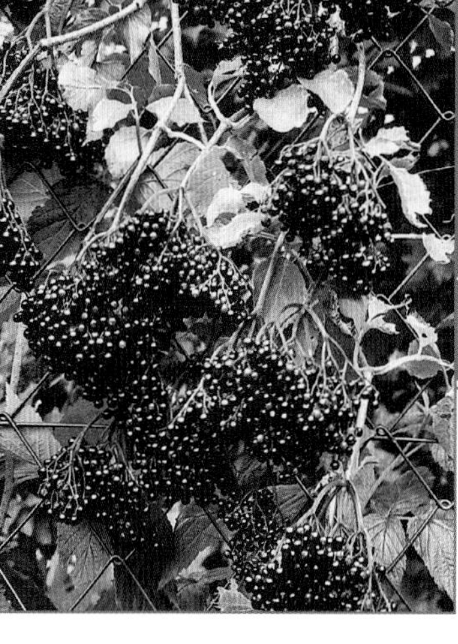

To achieve a clean, quality mash, the following additives are necessary:

- pure selected yeast
- pectin-degrading enzyme
- acidity adjusted to pH 3.0-3.2
- yeast salt (adding yeast salt is forbidden in Germany, check with your relevant local government agency regarding regulations on yeast salt)
- anti-foaming agent to prevent foaming during fermentation

Directions

First, because of the low acidity, the acidity must be adjusted (pH 3.0-3.2) and then yeast, enzyme, yeast salt, and anti-foaming agent are stirred or transferred in.

Distill the mash as soon as fermentation ends—do not store the mash.

Use an anti-foaming agent, as the mash tends to foam heavily during distillation.

The mash and fermentation temperature should be 64.4-68°F (18-20°C). Seal the container and insert the airlock. Fermentation takes 10 to 14 days. One can tell that it has ended when no more carbon dioxide is being released through the airlock. The elderberry mash should be distilled as soon as fermentation has ended. Test the degree of fermentation (pg. 68) to be certain.

For the newer varieties, the value of fermented mashes is between 2 and 3 %mas. Storing the mash any longer is problematic and can easily lead to a variety of problems. Use anti-foaming agent when distilling to prevent the mash from foaming and running over. The elderberry distillate starts out yellowish, but this is no defect. Distillation of the mash takes place as described on pg. 90. During the second distillation, one must apply heat very carefully to enable a clean separation of the head. By all means taste test when switching from fore-run to middle-run and from middle-run to after run. One should capture as many aromatics in the heart as possible.

When raw materials are in short supply, low wine can be preserved for the following year.

Considerations

With elderberries and Rowan berries one should ensure that sufficient fruit is available for mashing. As the alcohol yield is relatively low, it is better to have four rather than three first distillations for a second distillation. If, for example, one only has sufficient fruit for a first distillation, it is more advantageous to make a blended brandy. Mix the berries with pome fruits and declare the product a blended brandy (*e.g. Elderberry-Apple Brandy*). The respective fruit percentages can be stated on the label (*e.g. 70% apple, 30% elderberry*).

When dealing with a mixed mash, your alcohol tax may be calculated based on the fruit with the highest rate of yield. The mash quantities are such, however, that this is not a consideration.

The low wine from alcohol-poor mashes naturally has a lower alcohol content (10-15% ABV), therefore great care must be taken during the second distillation in order to obtain a sufficient quantity of heart. The switch to after-run is made at about 45% ABV, with frequent taste-testing to ensure quality.

Because of the low alcohol content, two distillations are necessary even with a column. All plates are blind switched.

The distillate should be stored in the dark at a temperature less than 68°F (20°C).

ROWAN BERRY BRANDY

The Rowan berries should be left on the tree for as long as possible; wild (*uncultivated*) Rowan berries should even be exposed to several frosts before picking. The sweet or Moravian Rowan berry is a popular food for birds, thus the picking deadline is based on when the birds begin eating the berries. If the fruit is not mashed immediately, it can be stored for 2-3 weeks, packed loosely in fruit crates.

Only the berries are mashed. The stems and twigs must be removed, as they give the brandy a bitter taste. There are various machines for removing the berries from the twigs. These can also be used for elderberries. For small quantities, the berries can also be cleaned over rabbit wire.

For mashing, the berries should be crushed or ground in a mash mill. The stones must not be broken, otherwise the bitter almond oil they contain can be turned into prussic acid during fermentation. Rowan berries contain the natural preservative sorbic acid, which also hampers the yeast and can complicate fermentation.

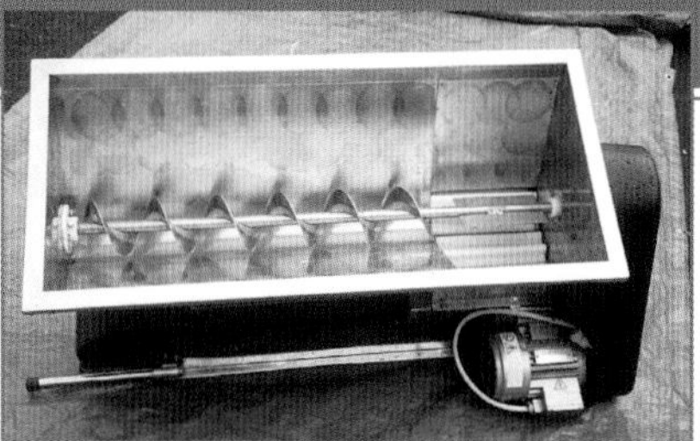

Stainless steel winnowing machine for Rowan berries and elderberries.

The following conditions are necessary for good fermentation:

- Twice the amount of pure selected yeast needed for pome fruits. It is a good idea to place the yeast in some fruit mash and leave it there for a day to multiply (*yeast pitching*). One to two liters of pitching mash should be added per hectoliter of Rowan berry mash.
- Add enzyme to liquefy the mash, two to three times the amount indicated for pome fruits (see pg. 48).
- Add yeast salt, as Rowan berries contain little nitrogen compounds, which the yeast definitely needs. Add 1.4 oz (40g) of yeast salt per hectoliter according to the directions for use (see pg. 55).

All three substances can be sprinkled onto the mash alternately or stirred into the mash.

As Rowan berries contain little juice, water must be added until all empty spaces are filled and the water just covers the mash.

Rowan berry mash is relatively dry, addition of water is necessary.

During fermentation a solid skin often forms, and this must be pierced now and then. To prevent this buildup one can cover the mash with a sieve cover and then weigh it down (*with a stone wrapped in foil or jug of water*) so that the juice is just visible. The cover material (*stainless steel or plastic*) must not release any material into the mash. Wood can transfer unwanted substances to the mash. The fermentation vessel must then be sealed as usual and fitted with an airlock.

Fermentation and Distillation

Rowan berries should be at a temperature of about 68°F (20°C) when mashed, so that fermentation begins immediately. Fermentation temperature is also 64.4-68°F (18-20°C). If pure selected yeast is not available, compressed yeast can also be used, adding 0.66-1.1 lbs/hl (300-500 g/hl). Stir the yeast into water with a temperature of about 77°F (25°C) and then mix into the mash. After the addition of yeast, the fermentation temperature should be 75.2-77°F (24-25°C).

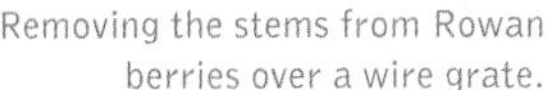
Removing the stems from Rowan berries over a wire grate.

In good conditions, fermentation takes 6-7 weeks. Definitely test the degree of fermentation (see pg. 68). Fermented mashes still have about 7% extract, measured with a saccharometer. As there are significant variations with this method, a fermentation test (see pg. 66) should be administered. If fermentation halts, start it up again by adding additional yeast. The mash should be distilled as described on page 90. Tasting should begin when the heart reaches 55% ABV. Rowan berry mashes often continue to produce good aromatic substances for a long time, therefore do not switch to after-run until tail substances are detected.

Beginning at 50% ABV, the distillate should be drawn off in portions (1/2 or 1 cup [1/8 or 1/4 liter] glasses depending on boiler size). It can then be taste-tested at leisure.

Store the heart as usual (see pg. 96). Rowan berry brandy adjusted to drinking strength should be stored at room temperature. In this way it ages much more quickly and becomes very smooth. A good Rowan berry brandy should have a strong aroma and taste and a tangy spiciness along with a subtle bitter almond aroma.

Long fermentation time and high remnant extract—test to determine end of fermentation.

First and second distillations are required even with a column, on account of the mash's low alcohol content.

QUINCE BRANDY

The quince is a well-known fruit in the Mediterranean region but also thrives in northern climates. Some cultures even take advantage of its fine, tangy aroma by placing ripe fruits in their wash baskets. In addition to its use in jellies and other delicacies, today the quince is also an interesting fruit for producing a delicious, aromatic brandy.

The flesh of the quince is very hard and stony and demands special handling prior to distillation.

After it has been harvested, the fruit should be left to ripen for two to three weeks. Use only fully-ripe and healthy fruit.

Before mashing, wash the fruit and remove all of the peel.

The following mash additives are required:

- Pure selected yeast—quantity and use as per the instructions on the yeast package.
- Enzyme to liquefy the mash. This is particularly important when using the relatively dry quince. Quantity and use as per the directions (see pg. 48).
- Acidification—adjust pH to 3.0-3.2 (see pg. 52).

If everything is ready, the fermentation vessel and airlock cleaned, the quinces washed, and the skins removed, mashing can now begin.

Mashing

Grind the quinces very finely and fill the fermentation vessel, simultaneously adding the enzyme and yeast. Leave a space at the top, seal, and let stand for a day, so that the enzyme can work and the mash becomes more liquid. Then slowly add the acid, stir well and adjust to pH 3.0-3.2 (see pg. 52 *for acid measurement*).

Dry fruit—add enzyme to liquefy the mash, distill as soon as fermentation ends.

Afterwards seal the fermentation vessel tight and insert the airlock so that fermentation can be checked. After one or two days, stir the mash well and check the pH value. The fermentation temperature should be 64.4-68° (18-20°C). When no more CO_2 leaves the airlock, carry out a sugar test to determine the degree of fermentation (see pg. 68). Distill the mash as soon as fermentation ends. A boiler with agitator is needed for distillation, because the mash is very viscous. Distill slowly and exercise care when separating the head, heart, and tail. Subsequent treatment as usual (*storage, filtration, etc.*).

APRICOT BRANDY

There are several things to be considered if one wishes to produce a high-quality apricot brandy. The biggest problem, surely, is procuring the necessary apricots. They should be healthy and ripe to overripe and have a variety-typical aroma.

Avoid breaking the stones during mashing, so that no prussic acid (*poisonous*) can form. One possibility is to remove some or all of the stones. It is up to the distiller

Good, aromatic apricot brandy requires sun-ripened fruit and proper processing.

to decide whether he wants some bitter almond tone (*from the stones*) or pure apricot aroma. It is sufficient if the apricots are squashed. If the stones have been removed the fruit can be finely mashed. Additives: enzyme to liquefy the mash and pure selected yeast (*each according to the accompanying instructions*).

In addition, acidification with an acid treatment is necessary, adjusting pH to 3-3.2 (*measure electronically*). Add the acid several hours after enzyme treatment, by then the mash will need more liquid. Fermentation temperature is between 57.2 and 68°F (14 and 20°C). Stir again after one or two days, but not again.

After two or three weeks, test the degree of fermentation (*see sugar test on* pg. 67). Storage after fermentation is risky. It is therefore better to distill the mash as soon as fermentation has ended. The mash must be stirred constantly during distillation.

Disposing of the Residue

1. The most ideal method of disposing of the residue is a line into a biogas plant. Energy is created and the by-product is an effective fertilizer.
2. Large-scale application to agricultural areas.
3. Into the sewers—approval is required from the district or water treatment facility. This is the poorest way of disposing of the residue.

Note

Feeding into public waters is strictly forbidden.

Table for Determining Actual Alcohol Content in Volume Percentage for Alcoholometers

	Temperature Fahrenheit (Celsius)										
Reading on Alcoholometer	41 (5)	42.8 (6)	44.6 (7)	46.4 (8)	48.2 (9)	50 (10)	51.8 (11)	53.6 (12)	55.4 (13)	57.2 (14)	59 (15)
35	41.1	40.7	40.3	39.9	39.5	39.1	38.7	38.3	37.9	37.4	37.0
36	42.1	41.7	41.3	40.9	40.5	40.1	39.7	39.3	38.8	38.4	38.0
37	43.1	42.7	42.3	41.9	41.5	41.1	40.6	40.2	39.8	39.4	39.0
38	44.0	43.6	43.2	42.8	42.4	42.0	41.6	41.2	40.8	40.4	40.0
39	45.0	44.6	44.2	43.8	43.4	43.0	42.6	42.2	41.8	41.4	41.0
40	45.9	45.5	45.1	44.8	44.4	44.0	43.6	43.2	42.8	42.4	42.0
41	46.9	46.5	46.1	45.7	45.3	44.9	44.5	44.2	43.8	43.4	43.0
42	47.8	47.4	47.1	46.7	46.3	45.9	45.5	45.1	44.7	44.4	44.0
43	48.8	48.4	48.0	47.6	47.3	46.9	46.5	46.1	45.7	45.3	44.9
44	49.7	49.3	49.0	48.6	48.2	47.8	47.5	47.1	46.7	46.3	45.9
45	50.7	50.3	49.9	49.6	49.2	48.8	48.4	48.1	47.7	47.3	46.9
46	51.6	51.3	50.9	50.5	50.2	49.8	49.4	49.0	48.7	48.3	47.9
47	52.6	52.2	51.8	51.5	51.1	50.7	50.4	50.0	49.6	49.3	48.9
48	53.5	53.2	52.8	52.4	52.1	51.7	51.4	51.0	50.6	50.2	49.9
49	54.5	54.1	53.8	53.4	53.1	52.7	52.3	52.0	51.6	51.2	50.9
50	55.4	55.1	54.7	54.4	54.0	53.7	53.3	52.9	52.6	52.2	51.8
51	56.4	56.1	55.7	55.3	55.0	54.6	54.3	53.9	53.6	53.2	52.8
52	57.4	57.0	56.7	56.3	56.0	55.6	55.3	54.9	54.5	54.2	53.8
53	58.3	58.0	57.6	57.3	56.9	56.6	56.2	55.9	55.5	55.2	54.8
54	59.3	58.9	58.6	58.3	57.9	57.6	57.2	56.9	56.5	56.1	55.8
55	60.2	59.9	59.6	59.2	58.9	58.5	58.2	57.8	57.5	57.1	56.8
56	61.2	60.9	60.5	60.2	59.9	59.4	59.2	58.8	58.5	58.1	57.8
57	62.2	61.8	61.5	61.2	60.8	60.5	60.1	59.8	59.5	59.1	58.8
58	63.1	62.8	62.5	62.1	61.8	61.5	61.1	60.8	60.4	60.1	59.7
59	64.1	63.8	63.4	63.1	62.8	62.4	62.1	61.8	61.4	61.1	60.7
60	65.1	64.7	64.4	64.1	63.8	63.4	63.1	62.7	62.4	62.1	61.7
61	66.0	65.7	65.4	65.1	64.7	64.4	64.1	63.7	63.4	63.1	62.7
62	67.0	66.7	66.4	66.0	65.7	65.4	65.0	64.7	64.4	64.0	63.7
63	68.0	67.7	67.3	67.0	66.7	66.3	66.0	65.7	65.4	65.0	64.7
64	68.9	68.6	68.3	68.0	67.7	67.3	67.0	66.7	66.3	66.0	65.7
65	69.9	69.6	69.3	68.9	68.6	68.3	68.0	67.7	67.3	67.0	66.7
66	70.9	70.6	70.2	69.9	69.6	69.3	69.0	68.6	68.3	68.0	67.7
67	71.8	71.5	71.2	70.9	70.6	70.3	69.9	69.6	69.3	69.0	68.6
68	72.8	72.5	72.2	71.9	71.5	71.2	70.9	70.6	70.3	70.0	69.6
69	73.8	73.5	73.1	72.8	72.5	72.2	71.9	71.6	71.3	70.9	70.6
70	74.7	74.4	74.1	73.8	73.5	73.2	72.9	72.6	72.2	71.9	71.6

with a Calibration temperature of 68° (20°C) (*Volume Concentration at 68°F (20°C)*).										
	Temperature Fahrenheit (Celsius)									
Reading on Alcoholometer	60.8 (16)	62.6 (17)	64.4 (18)	66.2 (19)	68 (20)	69.8 (21)	71.6 (22)	73.4 (23)	75.2 (24)	77 (25)
35	36.6	36.2	35.8	35.4	35.0	34.6	34.2	33.8	33.4	33.0
36	37.6	37.2	36.8	36.4	36.0	35.6	35.2	34.8	34.4	34.0
37	38.6	38.2	37.8	37.4	37.0	36.6	36.2	35.8	35.4	35.0
38	39.6	39.2	38.8	38.4	38.0	37.6	37.2	36.8	36.4	36.0
39	40.6	40.2	39.8	39.4	39.0	38.6	38.2	37.8	37.4	37.0
40	41.6	41.2	40.8	40.4	40.0	39.6	39.2	38.8	38.4	38.0
41	42.6	42.2	41.8	41.4	41.0	40.6	40.2	39.8	39.4	39.0
42	43.6	43.2	42.8	42.4	42.0	41.6	41.2	40.8	40.4	40.0
43	44.6	44.2	43.8	43.4	43.0	42.6	42.2	41.8	41.4	41.0
44	45.5	45.2	44.8	44.4	44.0	43.6	43.2	42.8	42.4	42.0
45	46.5	46.2	45.8	45.4	45.0	44.6	44.2	43.8	43.4	43.1
46	47.5	47.1	46.8	46.4	46.0	45.6	45.2	44.8	44.4	44.1
47	48.5	48.1	47.8	47.4	47.0	46.6	46.2	45.9	45.4	45.1
48	49.5	49.1	48.8	48.4	48.0	47.6	47.2	46.9	46.4	46.1
49	50.5	50.1	49.7	49.4	49.0	48.6	48.2	47.9	47.4	47.1
50	51.5	51.1	50.7	50.4	50.0	49.6	49.3	48.9	48.4	48.1
51	52.5	52.1	51.7	51.4	51.0	50.6	50.3	49.9	49.4	49.1
52	53.5	53.1	52.7	524	52.0	51.6	51.3	50.9	50.5	50.2
53	54.4	54.1	53.7	53.4	53.0	52.6	52.3	51.9	51.5	51.2
54	55.4	55.1	54.7	54.4	54.0	53.6	53.3	52.9	52.5	52.2
55	56.4	56.1	55.7	55.4	55.0	54.6	54.3	53.9	53.6	53.2
56	57.4	57.1	56.7	56.4	56.0	55.6	55.3	54.9	54.6	54.2
57	58.4	58.1	57.7	57.4	57.0	56.6	56.3	55.9	55.6	55.2
58	59.4	59.1	58.7	58.4	58.0	57.6	57.3	56.9	56.6	56.2
59	60.4	60.0	59.7	59.4	59.0	58.6	58.3	57.9	57.6	57.2
60	61.4	61.0	60.7	60.3	60.0	59.7	59.3	58.9	58.6	58.2
61	62.4	62.0	61.7	61.3	61.0	60.7	60.3	60.0	59.6	59.3
62	63.4	63.0	62.7	62.3	62.0	61.7	61.3	61.0	60.6	60.3
63	64.4	64.0	63.7	63.3	63.0	62.7	62.3	62.0	61.6	61.3
64	65.3	65.0	64.7	64.3	64.0	63.7	60.3	63.0	62.6	62.3
65	66.3	66.0	65.7	65.3	65.0	64.7	64.3	64.0	63.6	63.3
66	67.3	67.0	66.7	66.3	66.0	65.7	65.3	65.0	64.6	64.3
67	68.3	68.0	67.7	67.3	67.0	66.7	66.3	66.0	65.7	65.3
68	69.3	69.0	68.7	68.3	68.0	67.7	67.3	67.0	66.7	66.3
69	70.0	70.0	69.7	69.3	69.0	68.7	68.3	68.0	67.7	67.3
70	71.0	71.0	70.6	70.3	70.0	69.7	69.3	69.0	68.7	68.4

Example

The alcoholometer reading (*calibration temperature* 68°F [20° C]) for a certain distillate is 45% ABV at 59°F (15°C). The alcohol content at 68°F (20°C) can be determined as follows.

We find the number 45 in the left column (*"Reading on Alcoholometer"*) and move to the right to the column 59°F (5°C). The number there is 46.9, which means that the actual alcohol content at 68°F (20°C) is 46.9% ABV.

Example

The heart which is to be cut has an alcohol content of 64% ABV. The desired alcohol content is 45%. We search in the left column (alcohol content of the distillate to be thinned) for the number 64, and move across the lines to the column for the desired content (45% ABV). There we find the number 11.5 (43.7), which means that 11.5 gallons (43.7 liters) of water must be added to 26.4 gallons (100 liters) of 64% heart in order to achieve an alcohol content of 45% ABV (*also, see pg.113*).

Mixing Table for Cutting High-Percentage Distillates

	Alcohol Content % ABV, Desired Alcohol							
Content % ABV	34	35	36	37	38	39	40	41
79	36.1 (136.5)	34.3 (129.8)	32.6 (123.5)	31.1 (117.6)	29.6 (111.9)	28.1 (106.5)	26.8 (101.4)	25.5 (96.5)
78	35.2 (133.4)	33.5 (126.8)	31.8 (120.5)	30.3 (114.7)	28.8 (109.1)	27.4 (103.7)	26.1 (98.7)	24.8 (93.9)
77	34.4 (130.3)	32.7 (123.8)	31.1 (117.6)	29.5 (111.8)	28.1 (106.3)	26.7 (101)	25.4 (96)	24.1 (91.3)
76	33.6 (127.2)	31.9 (120.8)	30.3 (114.7)	28.8 (109)	27.3 (103.5)	26 (98.3)	24.7 (93.4)	23.4 (88.7)
75	32.8 (124.1)	31.1 (117.8)	29.5 (111.8)	28.1 (106.2)	26.6 (100.7)	25.3 (95.6)	24 (90.8)	22.7 (86.1)
74	32 (121)	30.3 (114.8)	28.7 (108.8)	27.3 (103.3)	25.9 (97.9)	24.5 (92.9)	23.3 (88.1)	22.1 (83.5)
73	31.1 (117.9)	29.5 (111.8)	28 (105.9)	26.5 (100.4)	25.1 (95.1)	23.8 (90.2)	22.6 (85.5)	21.4 (80.9)
72	30.4 (114.9)	28.7 (108.8)	27.2 (103)	25.8 (97.6)	24.4 (92.4)	23.1 (87.5)	21.9 (82.9)	20.7 (78.4)
71	29.5 (111.8)	27.9 (105.8)	26.4 (100.1)	25 (94.7)	23.7 (89.6)	22.4 (84.8)	21.2 (80.2)	20 (75.8)
70	28.7 (108.7)	27.2 (102.8)	25.7 (97.2)	24.3 (91.8)	22.9 (86.8)	21.7 (82.1)	20.5 (77.6)	19.3 (73.2)
69	27.9 (105.7)	26.4 (99.8)	24.9 (94.3)	23.5 (89.1)	22.2 (84.1)	21 (79.4)	19.8 (75)	18.7 (70.7)
68	27.1 (102.6)	25.6 (96.8)	24.1 (91.4)	22.8 (86.2)	21.5 (81.3)	20.3 (76.7)	19.1 (72.3)	18 (68.1)
67	26.3 (99.5)	24.8 (93.8)	23.4 (88.5)	22 (83.4)	20.8 (78.6)	19.5 (74)	18.4 (69.7)	17.3 (65.5)
66	25.5 (96.5)	24 (90.9)	22.6 (85.6)	21.3 (80.6)	20.1 (75.9)	18.9 (71.4)	17.7 (67.1)	16.6 (63)
65	24.7 (93.4)	23.2 (87.9)	21.8 (82.7)	20.6 (77.8)	19.3 (73.1)	18.1 (68.7)	17 (64.5)	16 (60.4)
64	23.8 (90.2)	22.4 (84.9)	21.1 (79.8)	19.8 (75)	18.6 (70.3)	17.4 (66)	16.4 (61.9)	15.3 (57.8)
63	23.1 (87.3)	21.6 (81.9)	20.3 (76.9)	19.1 (72.2)	17.9 (67.6)	16.7 (63.3)	15.7 (59.3)	14.6 (55.3)
62	22.3 (84.3)	20.9 (79)	19.5 (74)	18.3 (69.4)	17.1 (64.9)	16 (60.7)	15 (56.7)	13.9 (52.8)
61	21.5 (81.2)	20.1 (76)	18.8 (71.1)	17.6 (66.5)	16.4 (62.1)	15.3 (58)	14.3 (54.1)	13.3 (50.2)
60	20.7 (78.2)	19.3 (73)	18 (68.2)	16.8 (63.7)	15.7 (59.4)	14.6 (55.3)	13.6 (51.5)	12.6 (47.7)
59	19 (72)	17.7 (67.1)	16.5 (62.5)	15.3 (58.1)	14.2 (53.9)	13.2 (50)	12.2 (46.3)	11.3 (42.6)
58	19 (72)	17.7 (67.1)	16.5 (62.5)	15.3 (58.1)	14.2 (53.9)	13.2 (50)	12.2 (46.3)	11.3 (42.6)
57	18.2 (69)	16.9 (64.1)	15.8 (59.8)	14.6 (55.3)	13.5 (51.2)	12.5 (47.3)	11.5 (43.7)	10.6 (40.1)
56	17.4 (66)	16.2 (61.2)	15 (56.7)	13.9 (52.5)	12.8 (48.5)	11.8 (44.7)	10.9 (41.1)	9.9 (37.6)
55	16.6 (62.9)	15.4 (58.2)	14.2 (53.8)	13.1 (49.7)	12.1 (45.8)	11.1 (42)	10.1 (38.4)	9.2 (35)
54	15.8 (59.8)	14.6 (55.2)	13.4 (50.9)	12.4 (46.9)	11.4 (43)	10.4 (39.3)	9.5 (35.8)	8.6 (32.5)
53	15 (56.8)	13.8 (52.3)	12.7 (48)	11.6 (44.1)	10.6 (40.3)	9.7 (36.7)	8.8 (33.2)	7.9 (30)
52	14.1 (53.5)	13 (49.4)	11.9 (45.2)	10.9 (41.3)	9.9 (37.6)	9 (34.1)	8.1 (30.7)	7.3 (27.5)
51	13.4 (50.8)	12.3 (46.4)	11.2 (42.3)	10.2 (38.5)	9.2 (34.9)	8.3 (31.4)	7.4 (28.1)	6.6 (24.9)
50	12.6 (47.8)	11.5 (43.5)	10.4 (39.5)	9.4 (35.7)	8.5 (32.2)	7.6 (28.8)	6.7 (25.5)	6.0 (19.8)
49	11.8 (44.8)	10.7 (40.6)	9.7 (36.7)	8.7 (33)	7.8 (29.5)	6.9 (26.2)	6.1 (23)	5.3 (19.9)
48	11 (41.7)	9.9 (37.6)	8.9 (33.8)	8 (30.2)	7.1 (26.8)	6.2 (23.5)	5.4 (20.4)	4.6 (17.4)
47	10.2 (38.7)	9.2 (34.7)	8.2 (31)	7.2 (27.4)	6.4 (24.1)	5.5 (20.9)	4.7 (17.8)	3.9 (14.9)
46	9.4 (35.7)	8.4 (31.8)	7.4 (28.2)	6.5 (24.7)	5.7 (21.4)	4.8 (18.3)	4 (15.3)	3.3 (12.4)
45	8.7 (32.8)	7.6 (28.9)	6.7 (25.3)	5.8 (22)	4.9 (18.7)	4.1 (15.7)	3.4 (12.7)	2.6 (9.9)
44	7.9 (29.8)	6.9 (26)	5.9 (22.4)	5.1 (19.2)	4.2 (16)	3.4 (13)	2.7 (10.1)	2 (7.4)
43	7.1 (26.8)	6.1 (23.1)	5.2 (19.6)	4.3 (16.4)	3.5 (13.3)	2.7 (10.4)	2 (7.6)	1.3 (5)
42	6.3 (23.8)	5.3 (20.2)	4.4 (16.8)	3.6 (13.7)	2.8 (10.7)	2.1 (7.8)	1.3 (5.1)	0.7 (2.6)
41	5.5 (20.8)	4.6 (17.3)	3.7 (14)	2.9 (10.9)	2.1 (8)	1.4 (5.2)	0.7 (2.6)	
40	4.7 (17.8)	3.8 (14.4)	3 (11.2)	2.2 (8.2)	1.4 (5.3)	0.7 (2.6)		
39	3.9 (14.8)	3.1 (11.9)	2.2 (8.4)	1.5 (5.5)	0.7 (2.7)			

The table gives the number of gallons (*liters*) of water to be added to 26.4 gallons (*100 liters*) of distillate, in order to achieve the desired drinking strength.

Alcohol Content % ABV, Desired Alcohol									
42	43	44	45	46	47	48	49	50	51
24.3 (91.8)	23.1 (87.3)	22 (83.1)	20.9 (79)	19.8 (75.1)	18.8 (71.3)	17.9 (67.8)	17 (64.3)	16.1 (61)	15.3 (57.8)
23.6 (89.2)	22.4 (84.8)	21.3 (80.6)	20.2 (76.6)	19.2 (72.8)	18.2 (69)	17.3 (65.5)	16.4 (62.1)	15.5 (58.5)	14.7 (55.7
22.9 (86.7)	21.7 (82.3)	20.7 (78.2)	19.6 (74.2)	18.6 (70.5)	17.6 (66.7)	16.7 (63.3)	15.8 (59.9)	15 (56.7)	14.2 (53.6)
22.2 (84.2)	21.1 (79.9)	20 (75.8)	19 (71.9)	18 (68.2)	17 (64.5)	16.1 (61.1)	15.3 (57.8)	14.4 (54.6)	13.6 (51.5)
21.6 (81.7)	20.4 (77.4)	19.4 (73.4)	18.4 (69.5)	17.4 (65.9)	16.4 (62)	15.6 (58.9)	14.7 (55.6)	13.8 (52.4)	13 (49.4)
20.9 (79.2)	19.8 (74.9)	18.8 (71)	17.7 (67.1)	16.8 (63.6)	15.9 (60)	15 (56.7)	14.1 (53.4)	13.3 (50.3)	12.5 (47.3)
20.3 (76.7)	19.1 (72.4)	18.1 (68.6)	17.1 (64.8)	16.2 (61.3)	15.2 (57.7)	14.4 (54.4)	13.5 (51.2)	12.7 (48.2)	11.9 (45.2)
19.6 (74.2)	18.5 (70)	17.5 (66.2)	16.5 (62.5)	15.6 (59)	14.7 (55.5)	13.8 (52.3)	13 (49.1)	12.2 (46.1)	11.4 (43.2)
18.9 (71.6)	17.8 (67.5)	16.9 (63.8)	15.9 (60.1)	15 (56.7)	14.1 (53.2)	13.2 (50)	12.4 (46.9)	11.6 (43.9)	10.8 (41)
18.3 (69.1)	17.2 (65.1)	16.2 (61.4)	15.2 (57.7)	14.4 (54.4)	13.4 (50.9)	12.6 (47.8)	11.8 (44.7)	11 (41.8)	10.3 (39)
17.6 (66.6)	16.6 (62.7)	15.6 (59)	14.6 (55.4)	13.8 (52.1)	12.9 (48.7)	12 (45.6)	11.3 (42.6)	10.5 (39.7)	9.7 (36.9)
16.9 (64.1)	15.9 (60.2)	15 (56.6)	14 (53)	13.2 (49.8)	12.3 (46.5)	11.5 (43.4)	10.7 (40.4)	9.9 (37.6)	9.2 (34.8)
16.3 (61.6)	15.3 (57.8)	14.3 (54.2)	13.4 (50.7)	12.5 (47.5)	11.7 (44.2)	10.9 (41.2)	10.1 (38.3)	9.4 (35.5)	8.7 (32.8)
15.6 (59.1)	14.6 (55.4)	13.7 (51.9)	12.8 (48.4)	11.9 (45.2)	11.1 (42)	10.3 (39)	9.6 (36.2)	8.8 (33.4)	8.1 (30.8)
15 (56.6)	14 (52.9)	13.1 (49.5)	12.2 (46.1)	11.3 (42.9)	10.5 (39.8)	9.7 (36.8)	9 (34)	8.3 (31.3)	7.6 (28.7)
14.3 (54.1)	13.3 (50.4)	12.4 (47.1)	11.5 (43.7)	10.7 (40.6)	9.9 (37.5)	9.1 (34.6)	8.4 (31.8)	7.7 (29.2)	7 (26.6)
13.6 (51.6)	12.7 (48)	11.8 (44.7)	10.9 (41.4)	10.1 (38.3)	9.3 (35.3)	8.6 (32.4)	7.8 (29.7)	7.2 (27.1)	6.5 (24.5)
13 (49.2)	12 (45.6)	11.2 (42.3)	10.3 (39.1)	9.5 (36.1)	8.7 (33.1)	8 (30.3)	7.3 (27.6)	6.6 (25)	5.9 (22.5)
12.3 (46.7)	11.4 (43.1)	10.5 (39.9)	9.7 (36.8)	8.9 (33.8)	8.1 (30.8)	7.4 (28.1)	6.7 (25.4)	6 (22.9)	5.4 (20.4)
11.7 (44.2)	10.8 (40.7)	9.9 (37.5)	9.1 (34.5)	8.3 (31.5)	7.6 (28.6)	6.8 (25.9)	6.2 (23.3)	5.5 (20.8)	4.8 (18.3)
11 (41.7)	10.1 (38.3)	9.3 (35.2)	8.5 (32.2)	7.7 (29.3)	7 (26.4)	6.3 (23.8)	5.6 (21.2)	4.9 (18.7)	4.3 (16.3)
10.4 (39.2)	9.5 (35.9)	8.7 (32.8)	7.9 (29.8)	7.1 (27)	6.4 (24.2)	5.7 (21.6)	5 (19)	4.4 (16.6)	3.8 (14.2)
9.7 (36.7)	8.8 (33.5)	8 (30.4)	7.3 (27.5)	6.5 (24.7)	5.8 (22)	5.1 (19.4)	4.5 (16.9)	3.8 (14.5)	3.2 (12.2)
9.1 (34.3)	8.2 (31.1)	7.4 (28.1)	6.7 (25.2)	5.9 (22.5)	5.2 (19.8)	4.5 (17.2)	3.9 (14.8)	3.3 (12.4)	2.7 (10.2)
8.4 (31.8)	7.6 (28.7)	6.8 (25.7)	6 (22.9)	5.3 (20.2)	4.6 (17.5)	4 (15.1)	3.3 (12.6)	2.7 (10.3)	2.1 (8.1)
7.7 (29.3)	6.9 (26.3)	6.2 (23.3)	5.4 (20.6)	4.7 (17.9)	4 (15.3)	3.4 (12.9)	2.8 (10.5)	2.2 (8.2)	1.6 (6.1)
7.1 (26.8)	6.3 (23.9)	5.5 (21)	4.8 (18.3)	4.1 (15.6)	3.5 (13.1)	2.8 (10.7)	2.2 (8.4)	1.6 (6.2)	1.1 (4.1)
6.4 (24.4)	5.7 (21.5)	4.9 (18.7)	4.2 (16)	3.5 (13.4)	2.9 (10.9)	2.3 (8.6)	1.7 (6.3)	1.1 (4.2)	0.5 (2)
5.8 (21.9)	5 (19.1)	4.3 (16.3)	3.6 (13.7)	2.9 (11.1)	2.3 (8.7)	1.7 (6.4)	1.1 (4.3)	0.6 (2.1)	
5.2 (19.5)	4.4 (16.7)	3.7 (14)	3 (11.4)	2.4 (8.9)	1.7 (6.5)	1.1 (4.3)	0.6 (2.2)		
4.5 (17.1)	3.8 (14.3)	3.1 (11.7)	2.4 (9.1)	1.8 (6.7)	1.2 (4.4)	0.6 (2.2)			
3.9 (14.6)	3.1 (11.9)	2.5 (9.3)	1.8 (6.8)	1.2 (4.5)	0.6 (2.2)				
3.2 (12.1)	2.5 (9.5)	1.8 (7)	1.2 (4.5)	0.6 (2.3)					
2.6 (9.7)	1.9 (7.1)	1.2 (4.7)	0.6 (2.3)						
1.9 (7.3)	1.2 (4.7)	0.6 (2.3)							
1.3 (4.9)	0.6 (2.4)								
0.7 (2.5)									

Alcohol Conversion Table for the Indicated Contents in volume percentage (% ABV), mass percentage (%mas), grams per liter (g/l), and the density (g/cm³) of Corresponding Alcohol-Water Mixtures at 68°F (20°C).

%VOL.	%MAS	G/L	(68°F [20°C])	%VOL.	%MAS	G/L	(68°F [20°C])
26	21.2	205.2	0.9670	51	43.3	402.5	0.9282
27	22.1	213.1	0.9658	52	44.3	410.4	0.9261
28	22.9	221.0	0.9646	53	45.3	418.3	0.9241
29	23.8	228.9	0.9634	54	46.2	426.2	0.9221
30	24.6	236.8	0.9622	55	47.2	434.1	0.9199
31	25.5	244.7	0.9609	56	48.2	442.0	0.9178
32	26.4	252.6	0.9596	57	49.1	449.9	0.9157
33	27.2	260.5	0.9583	58	50.1	457.8	0.9135
34	28.0	268.4	0.9570	59	51.1	465.7	0.9113
35	28.9	276.2	0.9556	60	52.1	473.6	0.9091
36	29.8	284.1	0.9542	61	53.1	481.5	0.9069
37	30.6	292.0	0.9527	62	54.1	489.3	0.9046
38	31.5	299.9	0.9512	63	55.1	497.2	0.9023
39	32.4	307.8	0.9496	64	56.1	505.1	0.9000
40	33.3	315.7	0.9480	65	57.2	513.0	0.8976
41	34.2	323.6	0.9464	66	58.2	520.9	0.8953
42	35.1	331.5	0.9448	67	59.2	528.8	0.8929
43	36.0	339.4	0.9431	68	60.3	536.7	0.8905
44	36.9	347.3	0.9413	69	61.3	544.6	0.8880
45	37.8	355.2	0.9395	70	62.4	552.5	0.8856
46	38.7	363.1	0.9377	71	63.5	560.4	0.8830
47	39.6	371.0	0.9359	72	64.6	568.3	0.8805
48	40.6	378.8	0.9340	73	65.6	576.2	0.8780
49	41.5	386.7	0.9321	74	66.7	584.1	0.8754
50	42.4	394.6	0.9301	75	67.8	591.9	0.8728

Distilling Step by Step

Here are the most important steps of the schnapps distilling process summarized in brief bullet points.

Here are the most important steps of the schnapps-distilling process summarized in brief bullet points. Remember, before you can start these procedures you must make sure that you are in full compliance of your national and local laws regarding owning, registering, and operating a still to produce fruit brandy or any other type of alcohol.

1. Which types of fruit or other raw materials are available for distillation this year?
2. Procure, examine, and check the fermentation vessels in a timely manor.
3. Procure pure selected dry yeast, enzyme, acid, and yeast nutrient ahead of time.
4. Clean and check mash mill.
5. Assemble and prepare raw materials—only good, clean, rot-free raw materials produce a good brandy.
6. Thaw frozen or cold fruit, so that a mash temperature of at least 64.4°F (18°C) is achieved.
7. Mash the chopped or crushed fruit, adding yeast, enzyme, and possibly acid.
8. Seal the fermentation vessel.
9. Maintain a fermentation temperature of 64.4-68°F (18-20°C) so that fermentation does not become stuck. Williams Christ pears and raspberries have a maximum fermentation temperature of 64.4°F (18°C)
10. Report to related government agencies at the proper time before beginning fermentation
11. Fermentation takes 2-6 weeks. Watch for the end of fermentation—check with a saccharometer.
12. Distill the mash with a simple still or column.
13. First distillation.
14. Second distillation—the most important distillation—distill slowly and separate fore-run, middle-run, and after-run.
15. Prior to sale/distribution, determine the alcohol content and adjust to the proper drinking strength.
16. Age the heart and the finished brandy.

Distilling Terminology

After-Run (*Tail*)	Third part (*third fraction*) of the second distillation containing heavy volatiles such as higher alcohols.
Alcoholometer	Device for measuring the alcohol content of liquids.
Amylase	An enzyme that breaks sugar down into starch.
Brand	EU term for fruit brandy or schnapps.
Condensation	Liquefaction of vapor through cooling.
Distillation	Separation of volatile from non-volatile substances through heating (*evaporation*) and subsequent cooling
Distillate	The product of distillation (*runoff from cooler*).
Distillate	The drinkable part of the second distillation from the middle-run to the ready-to-drink brandy.
Enzyme (*Biocatalyst*)	Chemical agents that bring about chemical processes without being consumed.
Ethanol	Ethyl alcohol, potable alcohol.
Ethyl Alcohol	Potable alcohol, created by yeast from sugar.
First Distillation	First phase of the double-distillation process for the production of alcohol.
Fore-Run (*Head*)	First part (*first fraction*) of the second distillation, contains highly volatile substances.
Fractionated Distillation	Process which uses the different boiling points of substances to enable their removal.
Low Wine	Product of the first distillation.
Lutter Water	Residue left in the boiler after the second distillation.
Methanol	Methyl alcohol.
Middle-Run (*Heart*)	Second part (*second fraction*) of the second distillation, good distillate.

Plates	Elements which increase the alcohol content in a column.
Reflux Condenser	Cooler in the upper part of an enhancement column.
Saccharometer	Spindle for extract determination in fluids.
Second Distillation	The second distillation with simple stills, divided into the fore-run, middle-run, and after-run.
Slop	Residue left in the boiler after the first distillation.
Spirit (*Fruit Spirit*)	Unfermented fruit mashed in alcohol and distilled.

TERMS AND DESIGNATIONS

New Names and Terms	Formerly used Terms and Designations
Volume concentration in % (%vol)	Volume percent (Vol%)
Mass Content in % (%mas)	Percent by weight (Gew.%)
Liters of spirits of wine (l W)	Liters of spirits of wine (l W)
Liters of pure alcohol (l. r. A.)	Alcohol (A) Spirits of Wine (W)
Alcohol-Water Mixture (AWM)	Spirits

Legal Requirements in Other Countries

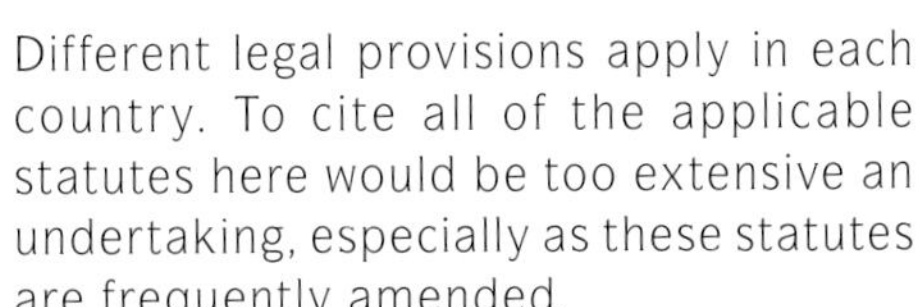

Different legal provisions apply in each country. To cite all of the applicable statutes here would be too extensive an undertaking, especially as these statutes are frequently amended.

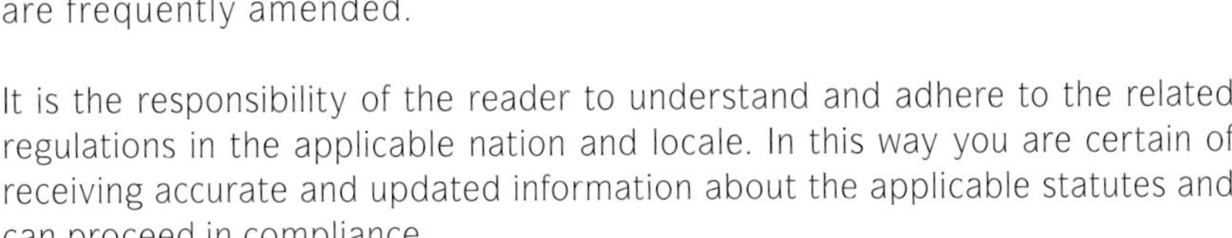

It is the responsibility of the reader to understand and adhere to the related regulations in the applicable nation and locale. In this way you are certain of receiving accurate and updated information about the applicable statutes and can proceed in compliance.

List of Tables

10 Rules for the Production of "Quality Brandy"

1

Use only ripe, healthy, and clean fruit. Dirt, mold, and rot lead to mash and distillate flaws.

2

Crush pome fruits and berries well; cores and stones must remain whole.

3

Use only clean, alcohol-resistant, food-safe, and well-sealed fermentation vessels with airlock.

4

For a clean, smooth fermentation, add pure selected yeast, enzyme, and, when necessary, acid to the mash.

5

Maintain a fermentation temperature of 60.8-68°F (16-20°C) (Williams Christ pears and raspberries 60.8-64.4°F (16-18°C). To allow fermentation to begin quickly, fruit should be at fermentation temperature when mashed.

6

Distill the mash when fermentation winds down or ends. If this is not possible, the mash must be stored properly.

7

Carry out the first fermentation quickly, the second distillation with a fine touch. Properly separate fore-run, middle-run, and after-run.

8

Store the heart in the dark, at 59-68°F (15-20°C) with exposure to air in storage containers. Berry brandies and Williams pears: at a maximum of 59°F (15°C) and full storage containers.

9

Add pure water to adjust the distillate to a reasonable drinking strength, filter if necessary, and age for a time.

10

Only make schnapps that has been distilled from 100% fruit and has no other additives.

Bibliography

H. Wüstenfeld, G. Haeseler. *Trinkbranntweine und Liköre,*
(Verlag Paul Parey, 1963).

Windisch, Rüdiger, Schwarz, Maisch. *Die Obstbrennerei,*
(Verlag Eugen Ulmer, 1923).

Pieper, Bruckmann, Kolb. *Technologie der Obstbrennerei,*
(Verlag Eugen Ulmer, 1993).

Physikalisch-Technische Bundesanstalt Braunschweig und Berlin und Bundesmonopolverwaltung für Branntwein,
(Offenbach/M., Amtliche Alkoholtafeln).

Tanner, Brunner. *Obstbrennerei heute,*
(Verlag Heller, Chemie- und Verwaltungsgesellschaft m. b. H, 1995).

Tanner, Brunner. *Obstbrennerei heute,*
(Verlag Heller, Schwäbisch-Hall, 2007).

Wilm Bartels. *Von der Frucht zum Destillat,*
(Verlag Heller, 2003).

Andreas Fischerauer. *Schnäpse und Edelbrände,*
(Österreichischer Agrarverlag, 2007).

Peter Jäger. *Das Handbuch der Edelbranntweine, Schnäpse, Liköre,*
(Leopold Stocker Verlag, 2006).

Alois Gölles. *Edelbrände,*
(Leopold Stocker Verlag, 1998).

Kleinbrennerei: Fachinformation für die Obst- und Getreidebrennerei

Appendix

PRODUCTION OF POTABLE SPIRITS FROM STARCHY RAW MATERIALS IN LICENSED GRAIN DISTILLERIES

by Peter Jäger
Austrian Beverage Institute, Vienna

INTRODUCTION

For the fruit distiller, the production of spirits from starchy raw materials is entirely new territory. Whereas the fermentable material, namely the sugar, is present in the ripe fruit, and thus in the mash, when working with starchy raw materials the starch must first be turned into fermentable sugar in a separate process. The more the better, meaning the better the alcohol yield. This process calls for great patience and experience. In this chapter I will explain the process of producing spirits from grain and offer an introduction to the practice.

RAW MATERIALS

The following table lists the most important raw materials with their starch content and alcohol yield.

Starch Content of Various Raw Materials and Alcohol Yield		
Material	% Starch	Liters of Alcohol/100kg
Rye	55-58	33-37
Wheat	57-60	34-38
Barley	53-57	33-36
Oats	50-54	31-33
Corn	58-62	36-38
Millet	58-62	36-38
Green Malt	35-40	22-26
Finished Malt	54-58	36-38

The alcohol yield in this table is the so-called "raw material yield," which means the number of liters of pure alcohol from 100kg of raw materials. This is only achieved at complete saccharification and includes the alcohol from the head, heart, and tail.

STARCH (*LATIN: AMYLUM*)

While starch is made up of simple sugar molecules, it cannot be directly fermented by yeast. It is therefore necessary to break down the starch into fermentable sugar. This process is called starch degradation (also starch gelatinization). The work is done by enzymes (see pg. 47). The enzymes in grain are not sufficient by themselves, therefore suitable enzyme preparations must be added.

ENZYME TREATMENT

Amylases are special enzymes for breaking down starches. Two different amylases are needed for starch saccharification: α (*alpha*) amylase and β (*beta*) amylase.

Enzyme Preparations

Malt

Malt is germinated barley, which is sometimes used green (*green malt*) but mostly dried (*kiln-dried malt*). The germination of the barley causes increased amounts of both amylases to be formed.

The enzyme's effect is dependent upon temperature, the pH value (*see pg. 51*) and the processing time.

It is important to note that the two amylases are most effective at different temperatures and pH levels. The optimal temperature for α amylase is 158-161.6°F (70-72°C) and it works very well at pH levels of 4.7-5.4. Levels below 4.2 are very bad, while temperature below 158°F (70°C) cause the process to slow down. The β amylase causes starch liquefaction.

The β amylase is damaged by temperature higher than 140°F (60°C). Its optimal temperature range is 122-140°F (50-60°C) and a pH level of 5.3-5.7. It is responsible for starch saccharification.

In order for both amylases to work satisfactorily and to avoid damage, a temperature of 131°F (55°C) to a maximum of 140°F (60°C) must be maintained, with a pH range of 5.3-5.7.

The main saccharification takes place in the mash tub. The presence of a certain amount of maltose (malt sugar) will to some degree check the work of the α amylase, however this will pick up again during fermentation if some of the maltose is fermented by the yeast.

Technical Enzyme Preparations

Technical enzyme preparations also contain two enzymes, however they must be added separately. The α amylase is added first at a temperature of 158-167°F (70-75°C) and a pH value of 5.5-5.7.

After the α amylase is added, temperature is maintained for about 10 minutes. The mixture is then cooled to 131-140°F (55-60°C) at a pH level of 5.3-5.7, after which the α glucosidase is added. This temperature is maintained for 20-30 minutes. After a positive iodine test (*pale yellow color*), the mixture is cooled to 86°F (30°C) and subsequently treated as per malt saccharification. The necessary enzyme amounts and handling procedures are contained in the directions accompanying the product.

The effective strength of each enzyme can be determined with the aid of an activity test. These can be carried out by any well-equipped laboratory. Tests on malt determine the activity of the α and β amylases. For technical enzymes, special tests measure enzyme units per gram or milliliter.

Alpha (α) Amylase Activity DBE in TS Malt	Rating
below 41	insufficient
41-52	adequate
53-64	good
over 64	very good

Beta (β) Amylase Activity WK Units in TS Malt	Rating
below 300	insufficient
300-350	satisfactory
351-400	good
401-450	very good
over 450	outstanding

CHECKING SACCHARIFICATION

In practice, an iodine test is used to check saccharification. The iodine solution used here should not be confused with the one used for treatment of wounds. It is instead an n/50 iodine-iodate solution which is available from specialty suppliers. This iodine solution causes pure starch to turn dark blue, almost black, while pure malt sugar turns yellow after the iodine solution is added. All intervening stages produce different colors. The intermediate products are called dextrins. The more the starch chains are attacked by the enzymes, the more the iodine test produces brownish to yellowish colors.

The following table summarizes iodine test color reactions

Saccharification Test (Iodine Test)			
Amylum Amylodextrin Erythrodextrin	(Starch) (Oligosaccaride) (intermediate stage)	Dark Blue Blue-Violet Red-Brown	Work of the α amylase
Achroodextrin Maktodextrin Maltose	(intermediate stage) (intermediate stage) (Sugar)	Yellowish/Red Brown Dark Yellow Bright Yellow	Work of the β amylase

Now the maltose can be fermented by the yeast.

TECHNOLOGY

The production of spirits from starchy raw materials takes place in the following stages:

- Preparatory work: grinding of the grain and malt (dry malt)
- Mash work: adjusting the pH level
  starch liquefaction (α *amylase effect*) and
  starch saccharification (β *amylase effect*)
- Addition of yeast, fermentation, distillation

MASHING PROCEDURE

Rural bonded distilleries employ the high-pressure steam method, so that optimal starch degradation as a basis for starch liquefaction and starch saccharification is achieved. Using this procedure, there is no requirement to grind the grain first. Temperature-wise, the process proceeds from top to bottom, meaning one employs a falling mash process in which the 212°F (100°C) hot mash is cooled by cooling coils in the mash tub and in which the necessary enzymes are added at the appropriate temperatures.

In most cases, small licensed distilleries have neither a damper nor—except in the rarest cases—a steam boiler. Consequently, with mash as a means of saccharification, they are forced to employ a less-favorable process, namely isothermic saccharification (saccharification at a constant temperature). In order to use technical enzymes, the falling mash procedure must be used, even by small, licensed distillers.

The following is a description of a simple mash procedure with mash saccharification that can be used in any simply-equipped grain distillery.

It is essential that all preparatory work be carried out in an exact and repeatable fashion.

- The grain should be crushed as finely as possible or, even better, ground. Hammer mills and corundum stone mills are both suitable for this task. The finer the grain is ground, the quicker the saccharification process.
- The malt used for the mash (kiln-dried malt) should also be ground as finely as possible.
- The mash tub, which should have an agitator and cooling coils, must be thoroughly cleaned and disinfected prior to mashing. As grain often produces glue-like substances that can smear the cooling surfaces and interior of the tub, possession of a steam blaster or at least a high-pressure cleaning device is advantageous.
- Calculate the amount of water required for the mashed unmalted grain and malt.
- One can calculate 79.25-92.46 gallons (300-350 l) of water for 220 lbs (100 kg) of unmalted grain and 22-33 lbs (10 -15 kg) of ground malt.
- The required quantity of water should be at hand in the form of hot water with a temperature of about 158°F (70°C).
- The first stage of the actual mashing process, namely the mashing, can now begin.
- Pour 1/3 of the necessary amount of water into the mash tub. The temperature of the water in the tub should be 140-143.6°F (60-62°C).
- Now slowly stir in the ground grain, avoiding the formation of lumps.
- Then slowly stir in the ground malt, again taking care to avoid lumps.
- It would be even better to first stir the ground malt into some warm water (*approx.* 104-129.2°F [40-54°C]) until smooth and then allow it to soak for about 15 minutes.
- The "malt mash" can then be gradually stirred into the unmalted grain mash.
- When mashing has ended, the temperature should be adjusted to 131-140°F (55-60°C).
- Immediately measure the pH level and, if necessary, adjust to the 5.3-5.7 range using sulfuric acid. Caution: there is a risk of chemical burn when using sulfuric acid!

A rule of thumb to bear in mind: 1/3 oz (10ml) of concentrated sulfuric acid produces a pH drop of about 0.2 units per 100 liters of mash. Concentrated sulfuric acid should never be poured directly into the mash. Instead it should be mixed in a liter of water and then added to the mash.

In order to avoid splashing caused by exothermic reactions, never pour water into the acid, instead always add water to acid.

A pH electrode can be used to measure the pH level of the mash, but so-called Lyphan Paper or pH paper can also be used (see pg. 51).

- From the time of stirring and pH setting, a saccharification break of about 30-40 minutes should be observed, during which the mash is constantly stirred. Care should be taken to ensure that temperature remains constant at 131-140°F (55-60°C).
- After 30 minutes, the first iodine test can be carried out. This is done by extracting a drop of mash from the tub with a thermometer and dripping it onto a piece of chalk. After the liquid enters the chalk it produces a brown patch, onto which a drop of the iodine solution is added. As soon as a yellow color appears instead of blue or red, the saccharification process can be seen as complete.
- If the results of the iodine test are positive, the mash can be cooled to 86°F (30°C) with the help of the cooling coil.

Before adding the yeast, determine the pH value of the mash once again. At the same time, about 1/8 gallon (1/2 liter) of mash can be filtered through a sock. In the filtrate, a spindle can be used to measure the extract value of the sweet mash.

- Now the yeast can be added. As a rule, 1/8-1/4 lb (50-100g) of baker's yeast is used per 26.4 gallons (100 liters) of mash. Before adding it to the mash, the yeast should be carefully crumbled into lukewarm water in a clean bowl and dissolved. The yeast suspension is then added to the warm, saccharificated mash, whose temperature is 86°F (30°C).
- Before cooling further, measure the pH value again. If it is higher than the 5.3-5.7 range, acidify once again with sulfuric acid.
- As there is always a serious risk of infection associated with rural operations, it is recommended that the grain mash be disinfected. As a rule, formalin (*formaldehyde*) is used for this. Based on a concentration of 35-40% formalin (*concentrate*), as a rule 0.67-0.84 oz (20-25ml) formalin per 26.4 gallons (100 l) of mash is sufficient. The formaline concentrate should also be thinned in water and then added to the mash while stirring constantly.
- Now, by engaging the cooling system, the actual fermentation temperature of 68-77°F (20-25°C) can be set.
- Before filling the fermentation tub or tanks, these—along with all lines, pumps, equipment, etc.—should be carefully cleaned (*lye*) and disinfected (*1-2% formalin solution*). A clean, low-microbial fermentation is only possible in clean vessels.

- After this preparatory work, the acidified mash (pH 5.3-5.7), to which the yeast has been added, can be poured into the fermentation tub (*stainless steel or plastic*).

As a rule, the entire mashing process takes 1-1 1/2 hours.

MASH TUB EQUIPMENT

In order to be able to properly process 220 lbs (100 kg) of ground grain and 22-33 lbs (10-15 kg) of ground malt, the mash tub's volume should be 158.5-185 gallons (600-700 liters). Equipment should include an angle thermometer or a PT 100 (*electric thermometer*) so that proper temperature can be maintained at the various stages (*saccharification, adding yeast, setting fermentation temperature*), as well as a sufficiently-long cooling coil made of copper or stainless steel, plus a flange-mounted pivoting stirrer (*propeller stirrer with a speed of 100-150 rpm*). To prevent rapid cooling of the mash and a drop in the proper saccharification temperature, it is recommended that the mash tub have a cover and an insulating outer wall. An adequately-large drain cock is very important, so that draining or emptying by pump can proceed quickly (NW 100-150).

If the mash tub has cooling coils, hot water can be run through them to heat up the tub. If this option is not available, the entire quantity of water can be added in several portions. The first portion's temperature should be 140°F (60°C) and the others should be sufficiently warm to maintain a mash temperature of 131-140°F (55-60°C).

PROCEDURE FOR FERMENTING SWEET MASHES

As a rule, temperature rises from the starting temperature of 68-77°F (20-25°C) to 86°F (30°C) in 24 hours. Assuming that saccharification was carried out correctly, fermentation usually takes 3-5 days. During this time, fermentation temperature can rise to 89.6-91.4°F (32-33°C) without presenting a danger to the yeast. Further saccharification takes place during fermentation, meaning—as previously mentioned—that the α amylase continues working to a degree as the maltose or glucose is fermented by the yeast. During fermentation the temperature and pH level should be measured and noted daily. The latter should never drop below 4.3.

After the end of fermentation, the product is referred to as "ripe mash." The ripe mash should be distilled as quickly as possible to avoid bacterial infections, loss of alcohol, and loss of flavor in the distillate. Therefore: report on a timely basis and distill as quickly as possible!

Before starting to distill, the following values should be entered in the journal: temperature, pH value, extract content, iodine test, and the alcohol content of the ripe mash, determined with the aid of a trial distillation. The following table illustrates the fermentation process during the course of a five-day fermentation, with values for extract, temperature, and pH value.

Fermentation Time in Hours	Extract % by Weight	pH Value	Temperature °F (°C)
0 "sweet mash"	14-16	5.3-5.7	73.4-77 (23-25)
24	6-8	5.3-5.5	82.4-89.6 (28-32)
48	2-3	5.0-5.3	86-89.6 (30-32)
72	0.8-1.0	4.8-5.0	77-86 (25-30)
96 "ripe mash"	0.5-0.6	4.5-4.8	68-77 (20-25)

During this time the alcohol content should have risen by 6-12% by volume.

YIELDS

Basically, one differentiates between the so-called "raw materials yield" and the so-called "starch yield." The former indicates the number of liters of pure alcohol gained from 100 kg of raw materials, the latter the number of liters of pure alcohol from 100 kg of starch. The starch yield is mainly used by rural bonded distilleries as an evaluation criteria for the distillation process. Rural small licensed distilleries usually calculate the raw materials yield. Depending on the process used, raw materials yields of 8-10 gallons (30-40 liters) of pure alcohol per 100 kg of raw materials can be achieved. This of course requires optimal saccharification work and an infection-free fermentation.

Fermentation Defect: formation of lactic, acetic, and butyric acid, or of mold. This causes the pH value to drop below 4.3. The mash is thus spoiled.

Defective Spirits: products derived from a defective fermentation.

What is in question here is total alcohol. Obviously the usable heart yields significantly less alcohol.

DISTILLATION

The distillation process is the same as in a fruit distillery. If a simple still is used, a raw brandy must be produced first and then a refined brandy. The latter is separated into head, heart, and tail. Proper separation can only be achieved through the senses (*nose and palate*). Basically there is no scheme for a certain quantity of head or at which concentration the switch should be made from fore-run to middle-run. This also applies to the after-run separation. Nevertheless, the following segment contains several guidelines for simple distilling systems. If systems with enhancements are used, refined brandy can be produced from the mash in a single process. The use of distillation technology with enhancement plates is, however, quite different than simple systems.

A certain amount of information is contained in the following paragraphs. Once again, I must stress that there is no scheme with respect to quantity or concentration for switching from fore-run to middle-run or middle-run to after-run and that the distiller must rely on his/her senses. Fractionation of the portions between the fore-run and middle-run and middle-run and after-run is recommended. This means that when the sharp fore-run smell begins to stop, capture 1/4-1/2 gallon (1-2 liters) of distillate in 3.38 oz (100 ml) fractions. The same is done at the beginning of the after-run. These fractions can be evaluated with the senses after distillation, so that one is in a position to determine the correct place to make the cut (*between fore-run and middle-run and middle-run and after-run*).

If the mash foams heavily, the addition of an anti-foaming agent such as silicon defoamer is recommended. A few cubic centimeters will suffice to ensure a foam-free distillation.

Basically, when using a simple still, the rule applies that the first distillation can be carried out quickly, while the second distillation should be done as slowly as possible so that the separations can be made as precisely as possible. The flow of distillate should be about roughly equivalent to the diameter of pencil lead.

Some distillers carry out fore-run and after-run separation during the first distillation. This is not absolutely necessary, however, as the important thing is proper separation during the second distillation.

Distillation Information for Simple Stills without Enhancements	
Alcohol Content... ...in the mash	6-12% vol.
...in the First Distillation Beginning Middle	 50-55% vol. 20-30% vol.
...in the Second Distillation Beginning Middle	 72-78% vol. 65-70% vol.

Time Required for First Distillation: 120-150 minutes

Time Required for Second Distillation: 240-270 minutes

Quantity Information: 26.4 gallons (100 l) of mash produces: approx. 6.6-8 gallons (25-30 l) of raw brandy

Fore-run during second distillation: 0.13-0.39 gallons (0.5-1.5 l)

After-run during second distillation: approx. 25% of the raw brandy

Switch to After-Run: Taste-testing or fractionating should begin at 60% vol.

Fore-Run: Can be used for liniments.

After-Run: Collect and distill again carefully.

Distillation Information for Stills with Enhancements	
Alcohol Content... ...in the Fore-Run ...in the Middle-Run ...in the After-Run	 80-85% vol. 65-70% vol. 25-30% vol.
Quantity of Head (Fore-Run)	0.26-0.66 gallons (1.0-2.5 l)
Switch to After-Run	Begin taste-testing at 60% vol.
Time Required for One Distillation	50-180 min. (First and second distillations in one process)

SLOP UTILIZATION AND WASTE WATER

Grain slop is a valued animal feed on account of its high nutritive value, and it is a valuable and popular supplement for cows, sheep, hogs, and also horses. The slop is used as a supplemental food, with a maximum of 8-10 gallons (30-40 liters) per day for cattle, 0.52-0.79 gallons (2-3 liters) per day for sheep and hogs, and 2.64-3.96 gallons (10-15 liters) per day for horses. It is important that it is given fresh and warm.

It is also important to check the pH of the slop. If the pH level is below 4.0, feed-lime must be added to raise the pH to 5-6. The slop should only be disposed of—thrown onto the manure pile or spread on the fields—if there is absolutely no further possibility of using it for feed.

Under no circumstances should the slop be introduced into waste water (*public sewerage system*), as it places too much pressure on the system. In addition, the solid contents create the danger of blockages in the sewerage system.

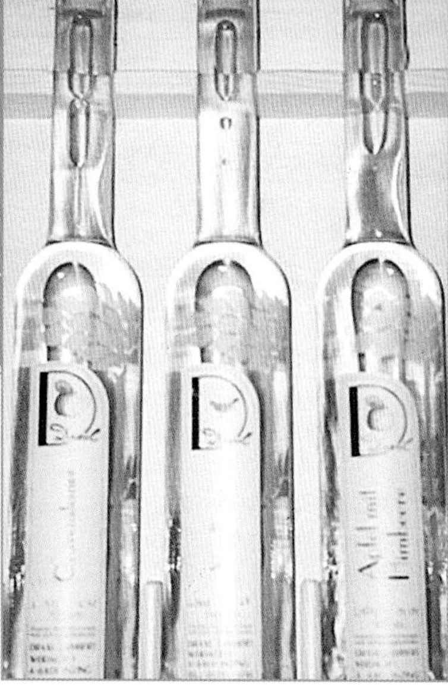

STORING AND AGING THE DISTILLATE

Corn or grain schnapps should be drunk as clear brandies, consequently aging in wood is not advisable. As a rule, corn schnapps is stored in glass, ceramic, or stainless steel containers. The minimum recommended aging period is 6-8 months. To avoid hazing in the bottle, the spirits should be cooled (32°F [0°C] *or lower*) and cold filtered before bottling.

MONITORING THE PROCESS

A certain minimum amount of testing equipment is required in order to closely monitor the fermentation and distillation processes. This equipment can be procured in specialty stores.

- Thermometer (*mercury, alcohol, electric thermometer PT 100*)
- pH device or pH strips
- Extract spindles (*saccharometers*) 0-5 %mas, 5-10 %mas., 10-20 %mas.
- Alcohol spindles 0-10 %vol., 10-50 %vol., 50-100 %vol.
- Filter and funnel for mash filtration
- n/50 iodine solution and porcelain bowls for iodine test
- Distillation testing device (1 l) with accessories
- Tables
- Literature

THE ENTIRE PROCESS STEP BY STEP

When Malt Is Used

- Secure all necessary certificates and licenses from the responsible government agencies and comply with all related national and local regulations
- Grind grain and malt
- Stir into water (131-140°F [55-60°C])
- Adjust pH level to 5.3-5.7
- Maintain temperature
- Iodine test until positive—bright yellow
- Cool to 86°F (30°C)
- Check pH, adjust if necessary
- Add yeast
- Add formaline
- Cool to 68-77° (20-25°C)
- Pour into cleaned, disinfected mash tub
- Fermentation—daily temperature and pH checks
- End of fermentation—immediate distillation

When Technical Enzymes Are Used

- Grind grain
- Stir into water (158-167°F [70-75°C])
- Adjust pH level to 5.5-5.7
- Add α amylase
- After 10 minutes cool to 131-140°F (55-60°C)
- Check pH to ensure reading of 5.3-5.7
- Add α glucosidase
- Iodine test until positive—bright yellow
- Cool to 86°F (30°C)
- Further processing as when malt is used

Index

A

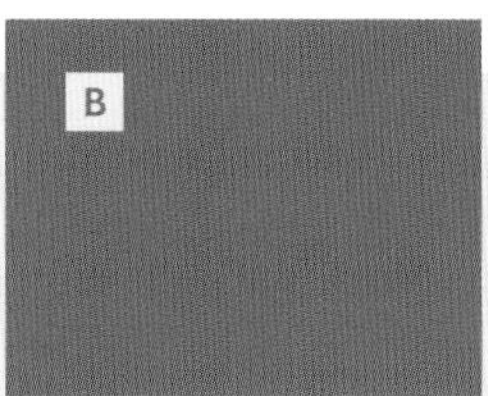
B

C

D

E

F

G

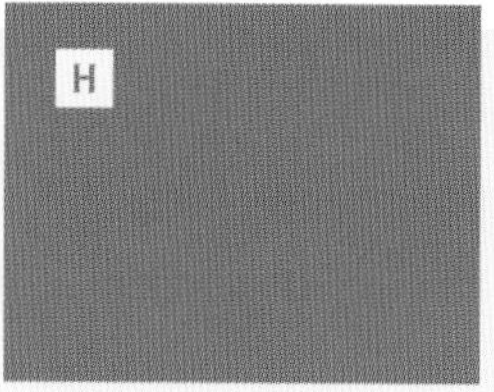
H

J

L

M

N

O

P

Q

R

S